GORDON

Mandarin and Pasha

By the same author

Gerald Sparrow

GORDON

Mandarin and Pasha

JARROLDS

JARROLDS PUBLISHERS (LONDON) LTD

178–202 Great Portland Street, London, W.1

AN IMPRINT OF THE   HUTCHINSON GROUP

London Melbourne Sydney
Auckland Bombay Toronto
Johannesburg New York

First published 1962

*This book has been set in Imprint type face. It has
been printed in Great Britain by The Anchor Press,
Ltd., in Tiptree, Essex, on Antique Wove paper.*

Dedications are unfashionable; nevertheless, I address this book in particular to young men and women, for if anyone ever answered the question 'How should I live my life?' it was Charles Gordon. I also hope that some of those who have served in the British Army may find this book worth reading.

I make no apology for the patriotism that pervades its pages. It describes a time when the British people had a good opinion of themselves.

Acknowledgments

Artists, including authors, are no longer fortunate in having a patron to encourage and protect them. The best modern substitute is a friend with a lively critical faculty. I have had this in William MacQuitty, who first suggested the writing of this book to me.

I am indebted to the Chamberlain of the Palace in Khartoum and the Officer of the Guard, to the Official in Charge of the House of the Kalifa, and to the Governor of the Red Seal Hills for courtesy and essential help.

I owe a particular debt to Brigadier F. C. Nottingham, the Commandant of the Gordon Boys' School at Woking, for allowing me to check facts I had unearthed in the Sudan in his museum and library. I am grateful to the B.B.C. for giving me an opportunity to broadcast on Gordon's telescope, and to the many correspondents who wrote me letters, as a result of that talk, containing new information on Gordon.

Contents

CONTENTS

Illustrations

Foreword

Victorian England was an age which nurtured and encouraged the soldier-mystic, and Charles George Gordon was, perhaps, the strangest, the most fascinating, and, in some respects, the most controversial of this rare breed of man, now, it seems, extinct.

If we give this man, at the height of his fame, his full titles—a Major-General in the British Army, a Mandarin of the Chinese Empire, and a Pasha of the Porte, we conjure up at once the outlandish romance which Gordon made his life. That he was a gifted soldier of exceptional personal magnetism is granted by his supporters and by his detractors. But this assessment brings us little nearer the man who has baffled all those who have written of him during his lifetime and since.

His biographers may have been mystified by Gordon but this did not prevent them from passing judgment on him. Perhaps because they were frustrated in the endeavour to reach Gordon the man, they arrived at two very different conclusions. The critical barometer fluctuated wildly between adulation and denigration.

Those who wrote of Gordon while the golden glow of his exploits was still alive concluded that there never had been a man who had given so much and accepted so little. He was: 'God's servant by election, God's image by beneficence.' 'Praise God', runs the inscription in the Cathedral Church of Khartoum, 'for Charles George Gordon, a servant of Jesus Christ whose labour was not in vain.' Gordon was the knight errant whom the British

Government could despatch to any corner of the globe where British interests were in jeopardy, in the assurance that, by his unique genius, he would set matters right. He is presented to us as an English gentleman and Christian in the best Victorian sense of the words, living by a simple code of behaviour based on honour.

The second view of Gordon is that advanced, with remarkably little evidence, by Lytton Strachey, in his *Eminent Victorians*, namely that Gordon was a homosexual, given to bouts of insobriety ('Give me my B and S'), and, morally at any rate, a fraud.

In this book I have suggested that both views of Gordon were and are false. I find that in Gordon we have a shy, sensitive man of exceptional brilliance—an introvert, dominated in his earliest days by his remarkable parents.

The view is advanced that Gordon, both in China and in the Sudan, was subjected to exceptional temptations—the temptation of unnatural love, the temptation of alcohol, and, in an almost biblical manner, the temptation of riches and power.

The circumstances of autocratic leadership, the very climate of China and the Sudan, greatly increased these temptations, and we are reaching for the key to Gordon's character when we realize that we are confronted by a man who is fighting his inner, spiritual battles at the same time that he is waging his public campaigns.

Out of all the struggle and the conflict emerges a great Englishman, or, as the devoted Scots would have it, a great Scotsman, whose interest lies largely in the way he won the private conflicts that at times tormented him.

If this is the right assessment of Gordon he is surely a more endearing and attractive character than either the Victorian saint or the humbug-sinner. I wait, with ill-concealed excitement, to discover whether those who read this book agree with my judgment.

I have delved, as deeply as I know how, into all the sources of information on this remarkable little man 'with eyes like blue diamonds'. The posthumous *Khartoum Journals* reveal a great deal, and nearly every letter and order reveals more. I spent months in Khartoum and Omdurman—they are now, for practical purposes, one city—and was given leave to work both in the Palace at Khartoum (where I discovered a Gordon telescope in the cellars) and in the House of the Kalifa. The photographs, with few exceptions, I took myself. I had the pleasure of meeting and talking to the present Mahdi, and I followed the trail of Gordon in the Sudan on his legendary travels by horse, on foot, by camel, and by river-boat.

In writing of 'Chinese Gordon' I found that the fact that I had lived amongst Chinese for many years, and had had dealings with them, made it easier to untangle the complicated, but fascinating, story of Gordon as a leader of the 'Ever Victorious Army'.

When I started to write I felt I knew Gordon better than my own brother, but whether I have been able to bring him to life for the public, as he really was, is for the readers of this book, and its critics, to say.

GERALD SPARROW

Khartoum-Omdurman, 1960
Suakin, 1961
Brighton, 1962

The chief characters who appear in this
book are:

CHARLES GEORGE GORDON

GENERAL GORDON, his father

MRS GORDON (née Enderby), his mother

LI-HUNG-CHANG, a Chinese mandarin

HANG-TSUE-CHUEN, leader of the Tai Ping rebellion

BURGEVINE, an American mercenary

THE EMPEROR OF CHINA

QUEEN VICTORIA

SIR EVELYN BARING (afterwards Lord Cromer)

THE KHEDIVE ISMAIL OF EGYPT

THE KHEDIVE TEWFIK OF EGYPT

THE MAHDI

ZOBEIR, an influential slave-dealer

SULEIMAN, son of Zobeir

COLONEL STEWART of the British Army

FRANK POWER, *The Times* correspondent in Khartoum

MAJOR HERBERT KITCHENER, afterwards Lord Kitchener

SLATIN PASHA, who became a Moslem

GESSI, Gordon's faithful Italian friend

Part One

I

The Young Gordon

THE career of the extraordinary man who is the subject of this biography—Charles George Gordon—falls, naturally, into two parts: his career in China—the epic story of 'Chinese Gordon'— and the even more famous story of Gordon in Equatoria and in the Sudan as Governor-General. Gordon's life, outside his Chinese and Sudanese activities, is not of major importance; indeed the episodes in the Crimea, in Bessarabia, in India, and in South Africa, seem, in perspective, to detract from the two great periods when Gordon made a reputation and created a legend that still lives.

There is an explanation why this should be so. In China, and even more in the Sudan, Gordon was to a large extent his own master, a condition essential to his unique gifts. He was a poor servant but a fine master. When for a few weeks he was appointed secretary to the Viceroy of India, Lord Ripon, the position was ludicrous. The gifts needed for that post—conformity, tact, a sense of protocol, and ingratiating manners—were just those gifts which Gordon did not have. He was a puckish individualist with great magnetism and—when he chose to exert it —charm, but he was never content unless he was on the bridge driving the ship forward by the light of Gordon.

Many young men are little influenced by their parents or their heritage. They break away when still quite young and by the time they are eighteen they have formed a new world of their own into which their parents may enter only on sufferance. But Charles Gordon was deeply influenced both by his father, against whose rigidity and conformity he rebelled, and by his mother, whose sense of adventure stirred the slim, fair youth, who was said to have a weak chest, but whose eyes were the eyes of a seer and of a practical prophet who intended to achieve fame in the explosive, expanding empire of Britain, by far the greatest dominion that the world had witnessed.

The Gordons were a family of soldiers and Charles's father, Major-General Henry William Gordon of the Royal Artillery, was a type that has now passed for ever, though as recently as twenty years ago such men, proud, shabby, and erect, could be seen in Cheltenham and in the warmer watering resorts of Devon and Cornwall. General Gordon was a bear of a man, with a great round head covered with thick black curls until he began to go bald. He had cheerfulness and the blunt candour of his type, and he had those china-blue eyes that could be so disconcerting when their steady gaze was turned on a delinquent. General Gordon believed in the Queen, in Britain, and in his regiment. He also believed in God and the Gordons. Had not his grandfather, David Gordon, been taken prisoner at Prestonpans while serving with the 47th Regiment? And had not his kinsman, Sir William Gordon of Park, fought for the Pretender on the same field?

After Culloden David Gordon and his son emigrated to America, where David died, but the son became a British officer, and his only surviving son was the Henry William we are discussing, Charles's father. General Gordon had a distinguished, uneventful career. The most remarkable step he ever took was to marry Elizabeth Enderby of Blackheath, by whom he had a large family—five sons and six daughters—the youngest of whom was Charles George. Perhaps because he was her youngest son his mother cherished him with particular affection and there is no doubt that it was she who lit a lamp in the mind of the young man that was never put out until he met his death, and was not, indeed, extinguished then.

Elizabeth Enderby came from a family of merchants, adventurers, and whalers who could have flourished only in the nineteenth century. Samuel Enderby, Elizabeth's father, was a London

city merchant, but he was a merchant of a unique category. He
was a shipowner and whaler, an explorer and adventurer. It was in
ships chartered from Enderby that the tea was taken to Boston to
be thrown into the harbour by the American rebels. Samuel
owned bottoms in New York and in Boston as well as in London,
and he, alone of shipowners at that time, was especially licensed
to take his ships in and out of all these ports and to all other parts
of the world—except the exclusive reserve of the East India
Company. Samuel was not a man of war. He did not, like Siamese
White, declare war on the Company. He avoided them, and after
the American Revolution used his fleets to round the Horn, to
chart the southern seas, and even to pursue whaling in Japanese
waters, as yet virtually unexplored.

The Government in London had ordered Botany Bay to be
surveyed as a penal colony, but the cost of transporting convicted
criminals to Australia worried them. They solved the problem
neatly by using Enderby ships, which made the outward journey
in ballast but returned with cargo. Samuel carried not only
convicts but free emigrants, and his ships played a part in opening
up the new continent of Australia and the green islands of New
Zealand.

With this background Elizabeth must, at times, have thought
her husband a little stuffy. His interminable harping on the
regiment, the fighting qualities of the British soldier, the eccen-
tricities and undesirability of all foreigners, and his irritating little
phrase 'Smart's the word, and smarter still the action', must, at
times, have made her want to throw something at him. She never
did. She was a Victorian wife: a gracious, comely creature with a
sense of humour, which she kept under strict control. She loved
her husband. He once had the grace to say to her: 'You have
been a lovely wife to me,' and, woman-like, she never forgot it.
But if she loved her husband in one way she loved Charles in
another. Her husband was strong, and narrow, and bigoted.
Charles was delicate, proud, temperamental. In her son Elizabeth
saw the seeds of greatness. This boy, she thought, could be a
Gordon *and* an Enderby—and what a combination that should
make!

The Gordons were not rich. They were described, in the odd

snob-language of the day, as being 'comfortably off, but not wealthy'. In fact they were a good deal less affluent than their friends suspected. Eleven children, even in those days, took a lot of educating, so we are not surprised to find Charles going to school[1] at Taunton, where his parents rightly thought he would receive as fine an education as was obtainable in England, almost free.

Charles made no mark of any kind on his school. But he lived those impressionable years in a town that teemed with the history of England, and it is fair to assume that so sensitive and perceptive a boy must have drunk in the atmosphere of great events that grew out of the cobbled streets of the borough market town. In Taunton a Saxon king had stood at bay. William of Normandy had built a castle here, and the doomed Duke of Monmouth had been proclaimed King of England in the Guildhall and had been greeted with wild enthusiasm by the crowds lining the Parade. Jeffreys had come to Taunton to smell out the traitors and to torture them with his tongue and his barbaric sentences. The story of Taunton was the story of marching men and violence, of rebellion and retribution, of war and of turmoil. The life of Charles Gordon was to hold all these things in abundance, and the story of England was to continue, rumbustious and un-predictable, in this schoolboy quietly preparing himself for life in the British Army.

We do not know whether Charles was consulted as to the career he wanted to follow. For a Gordon to go into the Army must have seemed as inevitable to General Gordon as the migration of the wealthy to Scotland after Cowes. But, certainly, if Charles and his mother had seriously objected they would have found some means of effective protest.

So the Taunton schoolboy was entered for the Royal Academy at Woolwich. After all, his father was a 'gunner'. There was no reason why Charles should not also enter the traditionally more intelligent side of an army career—the Royal Artillery or the Royal Engineers. He became, in fact, a Royal Engineer—a 'sapper'.

On the eve of Charles's departure for Woolwich, in 1851,

---

[1] This was before there was any desire by the fine old grammar schools of England to be regarded as 'public schools'.

General Gordon thought it his duty to give his youngest son a lecture on being an officer and a gentleman. He had no doubt that Charles, being a Gordon, would become both, but the young man of eighteen had shown distressing signs of outlandish originality that worried his father. He did not seem at home with girls of his age, preferring the company of older men; his views on social and political questions were almost radical, and he did not seem to share his father's suspicion of foreigners. . . . Charles stood respectfully listening to the long exhortation on duty and the spirit of the regiment. General Gordon, who spoke his mind on such occasions, must have made it clear that he was not altogether satisfied with his son, for Charles was on the verge of tears when, abruptly, he turned on his heel and raced upstairs to his bedroom.

There, in the evening, his mother went to talk to him, so that he should not take the admonition too much to heart. She sat on her son's bed as he drew the blinds. Charles got into bed and lay on his pillow. His mother said: 'Never forget, Charles, follow your own star. The world is your oyster. . . .'

He looked at her with those luminous eyes of his and answered: 'I shall remember. . . .'

Then, with that odd gift that was to stand him in good stead in many strange places and circumstances, he closed his eyes and with consummate ease achieved untroubled sleep.

2

Preparation

CHARLES GORDON passed through the Royal Academy at Woolwich creditably, but without outstanding distinction. It was characteristic of Gordon that only action brought out his gifts of leadership. He was a man who thrived on adversity. Trouble, difficulties, suspicions, danger—these were the flints that brought to life the flame in Gordon. In study and in repose he was no better than the next man, and a streak of hobgoblinish unpredictability in his make-up often worried his superiors.

Before we come to the exciting and strange events that made this young man a world figure as 'Chinese Gordon', we should know how his service abroad, before he was posted to China, seemed in retrospect to be planned preparation for what was to follow, both in China and in the Sudan. In fact, of course, it was the accident of circumstances and history that gave Charles Gordon the opportunity to become that valuable combination, the soldier-administrator, while still a very junior officer. And it is fair to say that the volatile and questing spirit of Gordon himself seized each opportunity as it arose, reaping the harvest of experience that a lazier or less able man might have ignored.

Circumstances were used by Gordon from the start. He refused to become their victim. This, his first appointment abroad after being commissioned, was to Corfu, a station that he did not want to revisit because there was no prospect of active service there, and because his father had served there when Gordon was a boy, and he already knew it well.

Gordon managed to dodge Corfu. There is no other word for it. Much greater latitude was allowed army officers at this time than is given them today. On coming out of Woolwich he had been sent to work on fortifications at the mouth of the Haven, being stationed at Pembroke. When the Corfu order reached him, in order to play for time he applied for two months' leave to be spent on duty in Pembroke. This was granted. Gordon's ambition was the Crimea and active service. He dreaded being sent to the West Indies even more than to Corfu. Early in December 1854 the demand for engineers in the Crimea became imperative and as if in answer to his prayers his route was changed. He was to proceed at once, with Major-General Keane, for the grim chaos that provoked the battles of Balaclava and Inkerman and the siege of Sebastopol.

It is typical of Gordon's career that he should find himself at the siege of Sebastopol. Years later, besieged himself in Khartoum, he was to make use not only of the techniques but also of the psychology of siege-warfare learned as a young lieutenant before Sebastopol.

His work consisted of linking up new British and French batteries and communications in advance of the front line and this led him frequently into danger. He makes light of it in his letters to his mother. With the exuberant optimism of youth it is plain that it never occurred to him that the light of Gordon might be extinguished before it had begun to shine.[1] His observations on his experiences are remarkably free of prejudice. He formed a high opinion of the fighting quality of the Russian soldier, but a less favourable impression of his French allies. As there were nearly eighty thousand French in the Crimea and less than twenty-five thousand British, the point was one of practical importance.

He speaks with sorrow of the death of Lord Raglan, beloved by his officers and men because of his generosity and kindness. He describes the fall of Sebastopol, and we get a first taste of the

---

[1] Charles Gordon always appeared to ignore personal danger, perhaps because he believed that courage is the profession of the soldier as piety is of the priest.

individual writing that was to make his *Khartoum Journals* a best-selling record.

'During the night of the 8th I heard a terrific explosion, and, on going down to the trenches at four in the morning, I saw a splendid sight. The whole of the Sebastopol was in flames, and every now and then terrific explosions took place which, in the rising sun, had the most beautiful effect. The Russians were leaving the town by the Bridge and all the three-deckers were sunk. . . .'

Gordon did well in the Crimea. Colonel Chesney, writing of Gordon's later career in China, says: 'He had seen war in the hard school of the black winter of the Crimea. At Sebastopol he managed to obtain a personal knowledge of the enemy's movements such as no other officer attained.'

The French, with whom he had maintained good relations (teaching several young officers English!), awarded him the Legion of Honour, a very rare award to a junior officer.

Gordon returned home, but in May 1856 he was appointed Assistant Commissioner to Major Stanton in Bessarabia to help in laying down the new frontiers of Russia, Turkey, and Roumania. This was Gordon's first taste, at the age of twenty-three, of administrative work. It took him to strange places; to Akerman, Bolgrad, Kotimore, Kichenev, Reni, Sratziga, and Jassy. He worked well and intelligently and was transferred to work out, on his own, the borders of the Asian side and in Armenia. He returned to attend a grand conference called in Constantinople and to make his report. He was sent again to Armenia, but this time as Commissioner. When he returned to England in the autumn of 1858 he was posted to Chatham as field-work instructor and adjutant.

There followed two years during which Charles Gordon reverted to doing the work and pursuing the life of a professional soldier of his day. It was the first of these periods of comparative obscurity that, throughout his career, are to form a strange, quiet contrast to the brilliant pattern of his life in its phases of eruption and activity.

In the summer of 1861 Gordon received orders that he was to proceed to Hong Kong, and in an exuberant letter to his family he shows the excitement and satisfaction that this news brought

him. Cathay instead of Chatham! What a change—for the better
—that was!

And when he arrived in Hong Kong, making the journey by
the all-British route of Malta, Aden, Ceylon, and Singapore,
he learned that several Englishmen, including a colleague, De
Norman, a Mr Parks and Mr Loch, as well as two army officers,
Anderson and Brabazon, with twelve others, had been taken
prisoners and were thought to be in the hands of Sankolinsin.

The arrest and maltreatment of British subjects at this time
was regarded as more important than any other consideration,
even trade, and the prompt reply of Britain and her French allies
was to invest Pekin, from whence the Emperor had escaped, and
demand the surrender of the city as well as £10,000 in cash for
each British subject taken and £500 for each native prisoner, and,
of course, the release of the prisoners.

The city fell, but the prisoners had died in torture. Their
wrists had been so tightly bound that the rope had eaten into the
rotting flesh. The fines were levied, and the Chinese were 'taught
a lesson'.

But the whole episode was for ever disfigured by the barbaric
looting and defiling of the Summer Palace. Gordon describing this
says: 'You can scarcely conceive the magnificence of this residence
nor the plunder and devastation the French had committed. . . .'

Gordon wrote fully of this amazing event and his powers of
description had matured since the day he wrote of the siege of
Sebastopol.

'On the 11th October we were sent down in a great hurry to
throw up works and batteries against the town, as the Chinese
refused to give up the gate we required them to surrender before
we would treat with them. They were also required to give up all
prisoners. You will be sorry to hear that the treatment they have
suffered has been very bad. Poor De Norman, who was with me
in Asia, is one of the victims. It appears that they were tied so
tight by the wrists that the flesh mortified, and they died in the
greatest torture. Up to the time that elapsed before they arrived
at the Summer Palace they were well treated, but then the ill-
treatment began. The Emperor is supposed to have been there at
the time.

'To go back to the work—the Chinese were given until twelve on the 13th to give up the gate. We made a lot of batteries, and everything was ready for the assault of the wall, which is battle-mented, and forty feet high, but of inferior masonry. At 11.30 p.m., however, the gate was opened, and we took possession; so our work was of no avail. The Chinese had then until the 23rd to think over our terms of treaty, and to pay up *£10,000 for each Englishman and £400 for each native soldier who died during their captivity*. This they did, and the money was paid and the treaty signed yesterday. I could not witness it, as all officers commanding companies were obliged to remain in camp. Owing to the ill-treatment the prisoners experienced at the Summer Palace, the General ordered it to be destroyed, and stuck up proclamations to say why it was ordered. We accordingly went out, and, after pillaging it, burned the whole place, destroying in a Vandal-like manner most valuable property, which could not be replaced for four millions. We got upwards of £48 apiece prize-money before we went out here; and although I have not as much as many, I have done well. Imagine D—— giving 16s. for a string of pearls which he sold the next day for £500. . . . The people are civil, but I think the grandees hate us, as they must after what we did to the Palace. You can scarcely imagine the beauty and magnificence of the places we burnt. It made one's heart sore to burn them; in fact, these palaces were so large, and we were so pressed for time, that we could not plunder them carefully. Quantities of gold ornaments were burned, considered as brass. It was wretchedly demoralizing work for an army. Everybody was wild for plunder.

'You would scarcely conceive the magnificence of this resi-dence or the tremendous devastation the French[1] have com-mitted. The throne and room were lined with ebony, carved in a marvellous way. There were huge mirrors of all shapes and kinds, clocks, watches, musical-boxes with puppets on them, magnificent china of every description, heaps and heaps of silks of all colours, embroidery, and as much splendour and civilization as you would see at Windsor; carved ivory screens, coral screens, large amounts of treasure, etc. The French have smashed everything in the most wanton way.' He adds:

[1] I can find no evidence that the French were more wanton than others.

'It was a scene of utter destruction which passes my description.' It is clear that the destruction of the Summer Palace was a deliberate reprisal. No doubt it confirmed the Chinese in their detestation of foreigners.

Perhaps in deference to his parents, Gordon omitted the part played by British troops in this horrible vandalism. But he does say that 'everybody' was wild for plunder.

Gordon soon found himself on active service[1] operating from the Taku forts, for China was in ferment. He starts to know China and its people and in graphic letters home he describes all he sees. But the challenge to the British, and to Gordon in particular, and indeed to the Chinese Dynasty and Emperor, came at this moment from one man, a village schoolmaster, Hang-Tsue-Chuen, who, declaring himself to be divinely inspired and destined to usurp the Dragon Throne, had gathered out of the red-dust villages of China a great and growing following, appointed four viceroys to surround him, and, with an army of fanatical followers and a bizarre perversion of the Christian faith, threatened to take over the Empire.

Gordon's life was to be the story of his will against that of two of these desert prophets, one in China and one in the Sudan. But in order to understand the nature and terror of the challenge of Hang-Tsue-Chuen it is necessary to know something of the background against which the Tai-Ping rebellion exploded and of the nature of the man and his message who inspired it.

---

[1] In view of the growing menace of the Tai-Ping rebels, Britain dropped her 'war' with the Emperor and acted as his ally.

3

China

GORDON had come to China at the most explosive and revolutionary era in its history. The events that occurred when he was serving in the Empire started a trend towards a communistic, as opposed to a dynastic, form of government and life. That trend was halted for a time, but the pattern had emerged and now in China we are witnessing the fruition of a way of life that has its roots in pride, poverty, famine, and ingrained distrust of foreigners.

So that we can understand the roots of the Tai-Ping rebellion that ravaged China, and the policies that made Gordon the head of the 'Ever Victorious Army' which, in the end, helped to crush the rebellion and restored the authority of the Emperor, an appreciation of Chinese mentality and character is necessary. Until the last year of the eighteenth century, when the Emperor Chien Lung died, foreign travellers in China were agreed that the peaceful and organized administration of the country was on a high level. It was a hierarchy that stretched down from the Emperor, through his viceroys to the mandarins, and, from them, to all the people. At this time, 'all the people' meant less than a hundred million Chinese. The dynamic, terrifying increase in population, accompanied by famine, was to take on its fiercest aspect during the next hundred years.

This old China was peaceful, enjoying a civilization in many respects far in advance of Western Europe. The history of Chinese art alone shows this, and the temper of the people was pacific, one of contentment and self-sufficiency.

A verse from the *Shih Ching* (the Book of Songs) of the Middle Ages reveals this. In translation it reads:

'Work, work from the rising sun
Till sunset comes and the day is done
I plough the sod
And harrow the clod
And meat and drink both come to me,
So what care I for the powers that be?'

True the Chinese traditional values were not the values of the Western civilization. We admired the successful merchant, they admired the scholar.[1] We, during the entire course of our history, have put our trust in force and the soldier. The Chinese despised both. It is fair to say that, by 1799, China had achieved a degree of real civilization far in advance of the Western nations who now began their penetration of her territory, and in advance we may reflect on the present age of the technocrat, in which we have discovered only the secret of destruction.

Absolute monarchy has much to recommend it as a form of government. There are virtually no 'politics' and so no politicians. The government of the nation can be carried on in a calm atmosphere with the ultimate good in view. It is not necessary to genuflect to popular opinion or passing passion, for popular opinion that does not favour the policies of the absolute ruler is treason. But there is one essential condition to good rule under absolutism. The man at the top must be genuinely interested in doing his best for his people, and his 'image' must be one that retains the respect of the people as a whole. The nineteenth-century emperors, on the whole, failed in this respect.

Chia Ching,[2] the successor to Chieng Lung, was neither dedicated nor wise. At a time when China needed ripe statesmanship to meet the challenge of unrest within and aggression from

---

[1] The word 'mandarin' is derived from the Sanskrit word for a scholar or thinker.

[2] These are Gordon's spellings of the Emperors' names. We now use: Kieng-Lung and Kia-K'ing.

C

without, Chia Ching[1] was concerned mainly with indulging his own appetites. Let us be fair and say that the temptations were very great. A succession of young women, and, if the Emperor was so inclined, young men, were constantly paraded before him, in case he should desire one of them. If he took a girl he could make her a queen or a concubine, he could strangle her, or have her eaten by ants. There were no limits placed on the attempts of the mandarins to please their master. Chia Ching did not give in to the worst excesses, but he was lazy and, worse, he was obstinate, and he would not take advice.

As soon as the people perceived that the Emperor was weak the country began to disrupt. Close students of China reporting home in the middle of the eighteenth century, and in the middle of the nineteenth century, present startlingly different pictures. In the first picture we are shown a happy, organized country, devoted to agriculture and the arts; in the second a nation torn by strife, with half a dozen bandit chiefs marauding, and with the age-old secret societies of China re-emerging.

It was against this background of disruption and dissolution, with the constant threat of the foreign powers who coveted the China trade, that the Tai-Ping rebellion broke out under the extraordinary man who became its leader.

Before the advent of Hang-Tsue-Chuen there had been ominous rumbles and revolts mainly, but not exclusively, in the south, which had a traditional dislike of the Northern Manchu Dynasty.

In Honan Province the White Feather and the White Lotus, secret societies with political aspirations, kept up a limited rebellion for the best part of ten years. The Triad Brotherhood— the triad represented heaven, earth, and man—having its roots in the south was even more ominous, for in its ranks, almost for the first time in 'recent' Chinese history, the discontented intelligentzia joined the mass of the people. The farmers were rebelling against corruption and tax extortion, the educated leaders were protesting against the usurpation by Manchu nominees of nearly all the higher offices.

Public office in China at this time was still very much sought

[1] 1795–1820.

after, not only because of its immense prestige but because of the revenue it brought in to supplement the slender official salaries. When the Chinese Minister of Foreign Affairs, years later, asked Lord Curzon, visiting China, whether his ministerial office provided him with adequate additional revenue outside his salary he was not being humorous. He was being inquisitive.

Hang-Tsue-Chuen was a Cantonese Haka from south-west China. He claimed gifts of divination and could put himself into a trance without difficulty. From the first he insisted that he had divine inspiration, that the Almighty was in constant converse with him, and that he was God's delegate on earth destined to sit on the Dragon Throne and bring peace and prosperity to the torn kingdom. This attitude was of course not new. Mohammed took up much the same position, but Hang-Tsue-Chuen's claim was new to this extent, that he founded his creed on Christianity, or at least on a strange perversion or interpretation of Christianity, which he had borrowed from American missionaries with whom he had been greatly impressed.

At first the Tai-Ping leader identified himself with the Triad Brotherhood, but soon he broke away and founded his own movement, which snowballed into a great revolution, culminating in his capture of Nanking which he held for eleven years, setting up a court of almost Imperial splendour. He was in fact the master of half civilized China and his writ ran to within fifty miles of the sea down the great fertile valley of the Yangtze. So that there were three powers in China. There was the official government of the Emperor, who claimed undisputed sovereignty of all China and expected tribute from many lesser states including Tibet, Siam, and what was to become 'Indo-China'. There was the Tai-Ping ruler in Nanking, defiant, and, apparently, securely entrenched. And there were the foreigners in the ports and coastal areas, growing ever stronger and more determined.

When the Tai-Ping rebellion became a serious menace there were many, including some of the ablest of the English observers, who thought that Hang-Tsue-Chuen represented a better prospect for China than did the corrupt and incurably indolent Hien-Feng,[1] but, on balance, although officially China was at war both

[1] Hien-Feng, 1850–61.

with Britain and France, the British Government decided to
support the Dynasty. Perhaps they perceived that the Tai-Pings,
whose social policies were very advanced, might lead to complete
social and structural revolution. If the old China they knew could
be shown up it was preferable to this dynamic new China which
they did not know, but feared.

An account of the extraordinary court of Hang-Tsue-Chuen
at his capital of Nanking is given to us by the missionary, Mr
L. C. Holmes. It is so graphic and observant that I quote it.

'At night we witnessed their worship. It occurred at the
beginning of their Sabbath, midnight of Friday. The place of
worship was the Chung Wang's private audience-room. He was
himself seated in the midst of his attendants—no females were
present. They first sang, or rather chanted; after which a written
prayer was read and burned by an officer, upon which they rose
and sang again, and then separated. The Chung Wang sent for
me again before he left his seat, and asked me if I understood their
mode of worship. I replied that I had just seen it for the first time.
He asked what our mode was. I replied that we endeavoured to
follow the rules laid down in the Scriptures, and thought all
departure therefrom to be erroneous. He then proceeded to
explain the ground upon which they departed from this rule.
The Tien Wang had been to heaven, he said, and had seen the
Heavenly Father. Our revelation had been handed down for
1,800 years. They had received a new, additional revelation; and
upon this they could adopt a different mode of worship. I replied
that if the Tien Wang had obtained a revelation we could deter-
mine its genuineness by comparing it with the Scriptures. If
they coincided they might be parts of the same; if not the new
revelation could not be true, as God did not change. He suggested
that there might be a sort of disparagement which was yet appropriate, as in the Chinese garment, which is buttoned at one side.
To this comparison I objected, as comparing a man's handicraft
with God's work. Ours were little and imperfect; His great and
glorious. We should compare God's works with each other. The
sun did not rise in the east today, and in the west tomorrow.
Winter and summer did not exchange their respective characters.
Neither would the Heavenly Father capriciously make a law at

one time and contradict it at another. His Majesty seemed rather disconcerted at thus being carried out of the usual track in which he was in the habit of discoursing, and we parted, proposing to talk further upon the subject at another time.' Mr Holmes continues:

'At daylight we started for the Tien Wang's palace. The procession was headed by a number of brilliantly coloured banners, after which followed a troop of armed soldiers; then came the Chung Wang in a large sedan, covered with yellow satin and embroidery, and borne by eight coolies; next came the foreigners on horseback, in company with the Chung Wang's chief officer, followed by a number of other officers on horseback. On our way several of the other kings who were in the city fell in ahead of us with similar retinues. Music added discord to the scene and curious gazers lined the streets on either side, who had no doubt seen kings before, but probably never witnessed such an apparition as that. . . . Reaching at length the palace of the Tien Wang, a large building resembling very much the nest of the Confucian temples, though of much greater size than these generally are, we entered the outer gate and proceeded to a large building to the eastward of the palace proper, and called the "Morning Palace". Here we were presented to the Tsau Wang and his son, with several others. After resting a little while, during which two of the attendants testified their familiarity with, and consequent irreverence for, the royal palace, by concluding a misunderstanding in fisticuffs, we proceeded to the audience-hall of the Tien Wang. I was here presented to the Tien Wang's two brothers, two nephews, and son-in-law, in addition to those whom I had before met at the Morning Palace. They were seated at the entrance of a deep recess, over the entrance of which was written, "Illustrious Heavenly Door". At the end of this recess, far within, was pointed out to us His Majesty Tien Wang's seat, which was as yet vacant. The company awaited for some time the arrival of the Western King, whose presence seemed to be necessary before they could proceed with the ceremonies. That dignitary, a boy of twelve or fourteen, directly made his appearance, and entering at the "Holy Heavenly Gate" took his place with the royal group. They then proceeded with their ceremonies as follows: First they knelt with their faces to the Tien Wang's seat and uttered a prayer to the Heavenly Brother; then, kneeling with their faces in the opposite direction, they prayed to the Heavenly Father; after which they again knelt with their faces to the Tien Wang's seat and in like manner repeated a prayer to him. They then concluded by singing in a standing position. A roast pig and the body of a goat were lying with other articles on tables in the outer court, and a fire was kept burning on a stone altar in front of the Tien Wang's seat, in a sort of court which intervened between it and the termination of the recess leading to it. He had not yet appeared, and though all waited for him for some time after the conclusion of the ceremonies he did not appear at all. He had probably changed his mind, concluding that it would be a bad precedent to allow a foreigner to see him without first signifying submission to him; or it may be that he did not mean to see me after learning the stubborn nature of our principles; but, anxious to have us carry away some account of the grandeur and magnificence of his court, had taken this mode of making an appropriate impression, leaving the imagination to supply the vacant chair which his own ample dimensions should have filled. We retired to the Morning Palace again, where kings, princes, foreigners, and all were called upon to ply the "nimble lads" upon a breakfast which had been prepared for us, after which we retired in the order in which we came.'

This was the great rebel court of China and it is obvious that, holding the very advanced views he did on social reform and land reform in particular, the Tien Wang, had he been able to usurp the Dragon Throne, would have become a socialist emperor, combining absolutism with a strange blend of dictated democracy. This was a realistic, not a fantastic, approach to power in China as it then was.

The Tien Wang had clearly taken over all the devices of the great man in China. The late arrival, or, better still, no arrival at all, was very much the Imperial trick for impressing greatness on lesser visitors. The Wangs, or viceroys, could be seen, but His Divinity could only be imagined.

The readiness of the Chung Wang to engage in theological discussion is typical of the old China, as is the underlying assumption that foreigners are always inferior, and usually wrong. During

Gordon's activities directed against the Tien Wang we get further glimpses of this man as he is corroded and corrupted by power and self-indulgence, but the missionary's impression of the vacant throne gives us the key to his character. He was the mystic who worshipped power, half genuine, half fraud. He became a god in his own vision.

The challenge of Hang-Tsue-Chuen was too brazen, too brilliant, and too dangerous for the Emperor to ignore. In desperation he turned to the foreigners for help.

This move by the Dragon Throne led to the recruitment of what was described, with suitable gravity, as the 'Ever Victorious Army'. For the part he played in training and eventually leading this remarkable regiment Gordon was to earn the popular title of 'Chinese Gordon' and, to his own dismay, to become a Mandarin of the Empire.

4

The 'Ever Victorious Army'

THE sacking and looting of the Summer Palace which, characteristically, Gordon had arrived in China in time to witness, was in some respects the end of an era. Although, in the Opium War of 1842 and in the Boxer rebellion, the peace of China was, for a time, shattered, on the whole, until the desecration of the Summer Palace, there had been a pattern of tranquillity in China as smooth, as orderly, and as ordained as the peony pattern of their eighteenth-century porcelain.

There was never again to be peace in China. For the next hundred years the country was to be convulsed by the growth of the Treaty Ports and foreign influence, by the rise of the war-lords, by the struggle of Chiang Kai-shek, by the barbarous Japanese invasions, and finally by the greatest convolution of all, resulting in the present form of extreme socialist government enforced by a powerful hierarchy who govern more ruthlessly than any emperor presumed to govern in the long and varied history of China.

The destruction of the Summer Palace also marked the high tide of foreign aggression in China. Until the Emperor's Marshal, Sankholin, had captured his foreign prisoners and they had died in captivity, Britain and France had been at war with the Imperial regime, but in the restrained manner of the day. We were always ready to talk things over if the Emperor would merely bargain from a position of equality. This was extremely difficult for him to do. Every Chinese dynasty, and the Manchus in particular, rested their claim to absolute authority on heavenly birth. The Emperor was God on earth and to expect him to receive foreign envoys and give them diplomatic immunity, to expect him to grant extra-territorial rights to foreign residents and to parley with ambassadors as if they represented states of equal importance to China, was asking a great deal.

The destruction of the Summer Palace, despicable though it was, compelled the Emperor to reckon with the foreigners as a power in China. He then had to choose whether they should be an enemy power or a friendly power, and he chose that they should be a friendly power because the Tai-Ping rebellion had mushroomed to such an extent that it represented an even more awful threat to all he stood for than the foreigners did.

When Hang-Tsue-Chuen started to have his visions and gather followers in Kwang-tung Province the Imperial Government were not unduly disturbed. They were accustomed to dealing with spiritual rebels. There were two alternative solutions. The most satisfactory was to defeat them in battle and to torture the leader publicly, taking out his eyes and chopping off his hands while he was forced to eat his own edicts. But this method had to be promptly instituted before the rebel became too strong. The second method was more British and less Chinese in character. The rebel was seduced. Friendly letters were sent to him hinting at the high regard of the Emperor, and the loyal mandarins were instructed to see that he had all the concubines—and opium— he might need. This was the Chinese equivalent to being created a peer in Britain, or a business ambassador in the United States, and very often it worked. The pampered rebel surrendered his morality and decided to live a life of luxury in the confines of his own palace and to press on no more with his dangerous mission.

In the case of Hang-Tsue-Chuen the authorities left matters far too late. Although he had started in a small way as a mere limb of the Triad movement, he grew unexpectedly rapidly until in 1852 we find him marching the thousand miles to Nanking, capturing it, and making it his permanent home and capital.

At first this strange man relied entirely on revelations which he claimed to have direct from God. He did not claim to be the

son of God. That position was already held by Christ. But he
claimed to be the brother of God and this was not intended as
blasphemy. In his later years he is quoted as saying that he himself would take the Dragon Throne, but in these earlier years he
said it was his purpose to oust the Manchus who were greatly
hated and bring back, in golden glory, the Ming Dynasty who,
although they had been fairly despotic in their day, now seemed
to the people to be infinitely desirable in comparison with the
Manchus.

Every enemy of the regime flocked to his standard, and even
the predatory war-lords, who from time to time pillaged the
suburbs of the great ports, thought it prudent to join him. His
army inspired terror as a matter of policy. Destruction in their
leader's name was their practice, and they tore the richer provinces
of China to pieces, pillaging to keep themselves fed.

Their appearance accentuated the terror. They wore their
hair long, not in pigtails but hanging down on to their shoulders
—an unheard-of insolence in China—and all their armies bore
banners proclaiming the invincible might of their leader and
recording his victories. When, with cries and beating of gongs,
these hordes arrived at a village, the quiet, close-shaven farmers
and peasants, who had been used to centuries of obedience to the
mandarins of the Emperor, quailed in fear before these savage
intruders. Every success that Hang-Tsue-Chuen achieved brought
him more and more followers.

But it was not until the capture of Nanking that the Imperial
Government were faced with a situation that could no longer be
ignored. The Emperor might keep his Foreign Secretary waiting
for days, he might ignore his Treasurer, but he could not turn a
blind eye to Sankholin who told him, in the flowery and obsequious phrases of the Palace Mandarin, the language of the
heaven-born, that the rebel had built himself a palace in Nanking
that threatened to rival in beauty and dignity the palaces of the
Dynasty and that, from the Porcelain Tower, there came a stream
of edicts assuming to rule all China, and promising the return of
the Ming Dynasty in its former might and majesty.

The conferences of the Imperial Court were never revealed
to the outside world. Often they took place at night by lamp-

light, the Emperor seated on his golden couch, the mandarins facing him in a circle kneeling on the carpets of the floor. But to one such conference, in fact the Chinese Cabinet in session, came the news that Hang-Tsue-Chuen had proclaimed himself the Heavenly King and had been acclaimed as such by the people. Moreover this upstart rebel had had the effrontery to ape majesty by appointing four minor kings—the Wang-Na, or Second King, the Kings of the East and the West, and the King in attendance, who was, in fact, a minister of the Royal Household. This duplication of the office of kingship was not confined to China but had spread into neighbouring countries. Even today the former palace of the Second King in Siam, now a museum, is known as the Wang-Na.

This was too much for the Emperor. He had to act and act now. The concubines were temporarily banished and for some months the Emperor devoted himself to affairs of State. It was necessary virtually to end his war with Britain and France and to concentrate on the extermination of this audacious usurper. It was not easy. But it could be done. The Emperor was helped in his determination to fight on one front only by the alarm that had spread into the large foreign communities in Shanghai where young Captain Gordon, R.E., was now stationed and carrying out his military duties.

The British Government might be very reluctant to help the Imperialists, but the rich merchants of Shanghai were determined to protect their city and a reasonable belt of the adjoining countryside, so that they would be able to carry on their profitable trade in opium, tea, rice, jade, and the other valuable products of China. The threat to them was the same threat that the Emperor faced. The Tai-Ping rebels were becoming daily more daring and new raids on quite a large scale deep into the Chinese suburbs of Shanghai were becoming far too common.

The mercantile community decided to organize their own defence force, and as a first step they commissioned two American gentlemen of fortune, Ward and Burgevine, to raise a regiment. This they did, and they even had some success against rebel bands. Unfortunately Ward died in action and Burgevine, who as we shall see was what would nowadays be called a gangster, was appointed to the command. However, Burgevine was not good at public relations. He especially objected to the dilatory way in which the Imperial Treasury paid himself and his troops. In the end, infuriated by this perpetual irritation, which he might have expected in Imperial China, he stormed a treasury, beating up the mandarins in charge. Helping himself to $40,000 he paid himself and his troops. But this was not to be tolerated. Dishonesty was not a major offence in the eyes of the Imperial authorities, but bad manners was almost a capital crime. To attack His Majesty's Treasurers was very bad manners indeed. Burgevine was dismissed in disgrace.

Li-Hung-Chang, the best governor that China had at this time, appealed to General Staveley to appoint a British officer to the vacant post. General Staveley looked around and his choice fell on the energetic engineer Captain Gordon, who was just completing a masterly survey of the thirty-mile area around Shanghai, which it was the original aim of both the British Government and the merchants to secure.

From this moment onwards Gordon becomes a factor in the affairs of China. His army linked to the Imperial Chinese Forces of the Emperor under Sankholin is to drive against the Tai-Ping rebels and in the end the 'Ever Victorious Army' is to be victorious in fact as well as in name. But we have by no means heard the last of Burgevine, and before he assumed this command Gordon served an interesting and varied apprenticeship.

China was a good station for the ambitious young British officer, but Shanghai, even at this time, was apt to seduce its foreign residents. True it had not become the sophisticated and immensely wealthy emporium into which it was to develop in the nineteen-twenties and thirties with the world's finest night-clubs and a startling collection of smart young Russian and Chinese women. But racing had already begun in a small way, and the British were starting their club-forming habits. Certainly Charles Gordon was not corrupted by the smiling blandishments of Shanghai. He remained that peculiarly British product, the adult male virgin, but he did not remain only that. He was also that fairly rare type, the dedicated professional soldier, intensely interested in people as well as terrain, the cultivated and observant engineer who could write arrestingly of all he saw and heard. This passage may evoke memories for foreigners who have loved China.

'The weather here is delightful; a fine, cold, clear air which is quite invigorating after the summer heats. There is very good pheasant-shooting in the half-populated districts, and some quail at uncertain times. It is extraordinary to see the quantity of fishing cormorants there are in the creeks. These cormorants are in flocks of forty or fifty, and the owner in a small canoe travels about in them. They fish three or four times a day and are encouraged by the shouts of their owners to dive. I have scarcely ever seen them come up without a fish in their beaks, which they swallow, but not for any distance for there is a ring to prevent it going down altogether. They get dreadful attacks of mumps, their throats being distended by the fish which are alive. The birds are hoisted into the boats, where they are very sick. Would you consider it a dainty dish?'

Life for Gordon was not all clear, crisp, Chinese winter mornings, shooting pheasant as one walked gingerly along the paddy-bunds. There was work to be done increasingly as the new menace of the Tai-Ping rebels stepped up their attacks, and looted and pillaged ever nearer Shanghai. The rebels had the advantage of extreme mobility. As Gordon put it, they could beat the foreign soldiers into a cocked hat when it came to putting in a sudden, terrifying appearance in force and then, having plundered and murdered, vanishing as quickly as they came. Partly this celerity of the rebels was due to the fact that they now wore distinguishing uniform. They were guerillas who could melt overnight into the civilian population, but even more it was due to their intimate knowledge of the countryside and their hardihood.

Gordon countered these disadvantages by himself getting to know every hill, creek, and village around Shanghai. Although chance appears to play a big part in the career of Charles Gordon, in fact it is usually his industry and his subsequent knowledge that promote the opportunities he seizes. He was the complete opposite to the pleasure-loving, womanizing, young army officer of his day. He was absorbed by soldiering. The problems which the effective defence of Shanghai presented fascinated him and their solution gave him personal pleasure.

In contrast to the magic mornings of the winter season the climate of the rest of the year was often horrible. Gordon describes a dust-storm that came up during operations he was engaged in at the Taku forts. The suddenness and strength of the desert onslaught was almost incredible. Sampans that had been gliding up wide creeks found themselves marooned on sand-dunes, the whole creek being obliterated. Sand entered one's eyes and one's nose, and the unfortunate men who were caught in the blizzard ate sand as well. After such a storm a man was red with the venom of the driven sand and exhausted to the point of collapse. But Gordon, who had come through the rigours of the Crimea, showed considerable agility and acumen in looking after himself and those for whom he was responsible.

On the 18th of August 1860 the Warrior King, one of the four Wangs, made a determined attack upon Shanghai, but was repulsed by the joint Imperial forces including the British and French foreign troops. The Wang tried again, but this time was more decisively defeated. Yet he was able to withdraw in good order to Soochow. Shortly after this the four Wangs joined in a great drive against the Imperial forces to clear for the rebels the whole Yangtze Valley between Nanking and Hankow.

This move deeply concerned the British, for they had treaty trading rights on the river. They sent Admiral Sir James Hope to negotiate with the Heavenly King at his palace in Nanking. The negotiations were protracted, as was usual in China, but the rebel emperor was finally willing to agree not to molest foreigners on the river, nor to attack Shanghai for one year. The Heavenly King did not want to fight on two fronts any more than did His Celestial Majesty, the Emperor.

This lull in hostilities enabled all the parties to take stock of their positions. But, at the end of the period of truce which the rebel king observed as he had promised, the British Government received a formal notice from Nanking stating that the agreed truce period had now expired and that it was the intention of the Heavenly King and his four satellite Wangs to storm and capture the city of Shanghai. This gentlemanly notification was taken

seriously by the British. Whereas up to now they had been doubtful allies of the Emperor, confining their interest to the protection
of the Treaty Ports, Shanghai in particular, now it appeared that,
to save China, both they and the Emperor would be committed
to a policy that aimed at smashing the Tai-Ping rebels. This, of
course, entailed military operations on a much larger scale, and
stretching over large areas of China.

The struggle was joined in earnest. It was to be a struggle to
the death and for survival. The Heavenly King had the Dragon
Throne to gain and his life to lose. The Emperor was challenged
as no Manchu emperor had been challenged before, by a determined and powerful adversary. The foreign commercial communities were deeply involved, for it looked as if a victory for the
Tai-Ping rebels would end the superior and special position of the
foreigner in China.

And for Charles Gordon, of course, this dramatic turn of
events was to be the flood-tide which might lead to disaster or to
fortune, for now Burgevine was cashiered in disgrace and Gordon
was to command the foreign troops of the 'Ever Victorious Army'
when, for the first time, they were to be tested in the burning
crucible of war.

5

Gordon Takes Command

YOUNG Captain Gordon was working on his survey some thirty miles from Shanghai when a messenger arrived bearing a letter from General Staveley, the British commander in that city.

Gordon, who had camped beneath the walls of a deserted monastery, told the messenger to rest and water his pony, which was exhausted, and to return with an answer in the evening.

The General's note was brief but friendly. Gordon was to report to him at once on a matter of major importance. As soon as he read the note, written in the General's firm, blunt hand, Gordon suspected that he was to replace the disgraced Burgevine. That, he reflected, would change everything. His survey, with which he had fallen in love, would still be very useful, but a cold wind of change was blowing through China. It was now no longer a question of holding Shanghai and clearing the environs of rebels. The rebels themselves would have to be smashed everywhere and eventually their capital must be taken. This was major war, and would provide countless opportunities for success or dismal failure.

Gordon had some hours for reflection. The messenger was sleeping huddled under the monastery wall, his pony tethered and resting a few yards away. These China ponies, though often no more than twelve hands, were tough, and this little beast, surefooted and intelligent, was to take his master back the thirty-odd miles to the city as soon as the heat of the midday sun had diminished.

Gordon's servant brought his midday meal. He was eating off the country now and there were three dishes: one contained rice which was steaming and beautifully cooked, each grain an entity, but the whole cooked with the cunning that the Chinese had for their staple food. The second dish was vegetable,[1] a green herb that grew along the disused canal that ran from the monastery to a village three miles away, and the third dish contained stewed ducks' feet. His servant carried a collection of these, dried, in a haversack. They were supposed to be a delicacy for his British master. At first Gordon had thought them revolting —when stewed the feet and claws would swell up looking like the boiled hands of a newly born baby. But by now Gordon had developed an appetite for Chinese cooking, with its bitter-sweet refrain and its infinite variety. He sent the messenger a bowl of rice and some dried fish and, when he had finished his eating, called him.

The man stood silently, holding the pony's halter, waiting for Gordon to hand him the message. Gordon scribbled a note saying that he was packing up and would reach the General in the morning. The dust rose behind the messenger as he cantered away and Gordon was once again alone with his thoughts. If the summons implied what he thought it did, what should he do? Must he accept immediately? Or could he ask for time to complete his survey? He decided to ask, in the strongest terms, for time to complete the survey on the ground that if not completed it would be wasted, but that when it was finished it would be of the greatest value in the defence of Shanghai.

Gordon thought that Staveley might counter this by saying that the objective had now been altered, the defence of the great trading city was no longer enough—the Tai-Ping rebels must be smashed, and Gordon must play a role in that drama. But Gordon though it quite likely that, if he played his cards cleverly, he might be allowed to finish his survey on which he had set his heart.

Gordon completed his packing that night. Before going to sleep he placed two of his men on guard as usual, said his prayers

---

[1] What Gordon's cook had gathered for his master was apparently *chue shai*, Chinese watercress.

D

—a habit that he continued all his life—and drank a glass of brandy-and-water. This was an innovation for Gordon. He had not drunk at all in the Crimea, but in China he formed the habit, and felt that he could not sleep so well unless he had his nightcap. Next day he rode back to Shanghai and in the early evening the General received him.

General Staveley was a man of few words. He came to the point immediately:

'Sit down. Li-Hung-Chang, the Governor, has asked me to put forward an officer to take the place of that blackguard Burgevine, to command the "Ever Victorious Army". You will be my nomination. You serve under Li. He is appointed by the Emperor's Marshal, Tseng-Kwo-Fan. Your orders will be to smash the Tai-Ping rebellion. You will have under you four thousand of the worst-disciplined Chinese troops in the world, who until now have been paid in drink, women, and opium.[1] You will have perhaps five siege guns, some cavalry, and an army of camp followers, wives, prostitutes, cooks, and coolies. It is the most challenging command I have ever had to offer anyone. What do you say? Will you take it? I am not going to insist. For a young man it may be too great a burden. Let me know tomorrow.'

Gordon saluted, dismissed. He had had no chance of playing his hand, but next day the General sat waiting for his reply. Gordon said that he thought he should complete his survey. The smashing of the rebels, the new objective, was going to be a long business. It would take two or three years, involving major engagements. If the survey was complete Gordon thought that the Shanghai garrison would have a plan whereby they could stop infiltration into the city by rebels.

The General hesitated. 'You wish us to make a temporary appointment until you have completed your survey?'

This had not occurred to Gordon. A temporary appointment would mean that he was definitely committed to take over as

---

[1] Under Burgevine these rewards for valour were highly organized. The Army had its own distilleries for the brewing of a potent rice-spirit with a high alcoholic content. Opium was seized from the owners if in its prepared form wherever the 'Ever Victorious Army' went, and the concubines of any city that was captured were herded into what was called among the junior officers the 'passion pen'. Age limits were fixed at fourteen to twenty-four. The concubines were preferred by the officers to the 'kiss-kiss' girls of Shanghai.

soon as he had completed his survey mission, which would be quite soon. But there was no escaping. He said: 'Yes, sir.'

'Very well. So be it. But do not take too long.'

Gordon had gained a respite, but from now on he knew that he was to play a part in the history of China. As well as completing a masterly survey he devoted his evenings to studying the larger issues of the rebel domains, their infiltration down the Yangtze, and the methods of war they used.

He found that, as well as the great area under their absolute authority, the rebels were terrifying half China by sudden appearances in force, intense spasms of plundering and torture, followed by their vanishing technique when they thought that the Imperial troops were approaching. Then they melted away as if some friendly conjurer had waved his wand over them. They inspired terror wherever they went; if a mandarin or headman failed to comply with their wishes they would disembowel him and stuff him with straw. Oddly enough this did not immediately kill the man. He was a ghastly, empty mockery, but he could give orders for some hours at least. The orders which the stuffed mandarins gave were the orders that the rebels dictated. Crucifixion was another common rebel practice, and the carving off of the victim's skin.[1] This was done almost as a ritual, each knife used in the process being numbered and marked for the operation it was to perform. It was a reign of terror.

Gordon reflected on this horror and thought that the rebels must be making many enemies but few friends, a fact he was to take full advantage of later.

Meanwhile a Captain Holland of the Marines had been appointed to temporary command of the 'Ever Victorious Army'. Holland was a brave and confident young officer, but he was brash and impetuous. This led to perhaps the greatest disaster that the Imperialists suffered, and a major victory for the Tai-Ping rebels. It also greatly strengthened Gordon's position when he took over the command.

Captain Holland started his brief career as a commander by

---

[1] The punishment of the thousand knives was very ancient in China. Those who performed the delicate and intricate operations demanded by this form of torture were adept in skinning a man alive. But, of course, the victim died later in agony.

deciding to take the rebel stronghold of Taitsan at all costs.

Captain Holland had a considerable force under his command for the operation he had in mind. Two thousand five hundred men of the 'Ever Victorious Army', now about to suffer its most humiliating defeat, more than five thousand Imperial troops, and two pieces of ordnance. It was perhaps typical of Captain Holland that his intelligence was disastrously inaccurate. He was assured, by supposedly friendly mandarins, that Taitsan was surrounded by a dry ditch that would present no real obstacle to his storming troops. In China dry ditches very quickly become deep moats and revert again to negligible obstacles according to the rainfall. When Holland's men attacked they found a deep moat which was quite impassable. They managed to throw a ladder[1] over it and across this they swarmed, but the weight of the men was too great and it broke. This led to utter confusion, and it is no wonder that the rebels exulted when they saw and seized their opportunity. One rebel scribe wrote of these events and his joy at the rout of the foreigners and their 'Imperial imps' comes through to us. It was a famous victory.

'Oh, how we laughed on the morning of the assault, as they advanced nearer to the creek which they brought no bridges to throw over! How we laughed when we saw their ladder getting weaker and weaker beneath them, and at last crashing into the creek! Leaving half the invaders on one side and half on the other. . . .

'So we laughed and so we jested as we saw the slaves of the Tartar usurper advancing to destruction. But our Lord was wroth: "Do they think us cowards," he said, "that they bring their hundreds against our thousands? Cowards even as the impish soldiers of the mandarins?

' "Arise," he shouted, "oh, inheritors of the Eternal Peace, and drive the infidels from the face of the earth." We arose as one man, crying blood, and the lust for blood consumed us like a ravaging thirst.

[1] A scaling-ladder. Captain Holland seems to have been incredibly rash and stupid to suppose that he could cross his men on one such ladder. No wonder the rebels laughed. The incident gives support to the view that one of the reasons for Gordon's extraordinary advancement was that he was a professional soldier among amateurs who did not take the strategy or tactics of battle seriously.

'Oh, how they ran! Yes even the English officers, too, ran as if the devil pursued them, though some fought bravely to remove their two big guns. But, would you believe it, they moved their small pieces first instead of leaving them to protect their heavy cannon. Oh, recorder of events, few victories have been as sweet as this!'

The reverberations of this military disaster went around China.[1] The King of the Eternal Peace exulted in his ivory tower. The Emperor in Pekin had anxious days and nights. What had begun as just another local revolt had swollen into a dagger pointed at the heart of the Imperial Throne.

Not only the rival kings were affected, the merchants in Shanghai and the coastal ports heard the news with dismay. At this fateful moment in Chinese history it really looked as if the Manchu Dynasty and the foreigners were doomed in China.

General Brown, who had taken the place of General Staveley, acted promptly. He insisted on Gordon sending in his report as it was, and taking immediate command. Gordon asked what his mission was. The General answered as briefly: 'To save China,' he said.

So, on the 26th of March 1863, at the age of thirty, Gordon stepped on to the stage, his mission being to break the Tai-Ping rebellion and to restore the Imperial power to all China, thus securing to the foreign powers the 'rights' that they had won by war, by negotiation, and by purchase. It was a task of herculean dimensions. Hannibal had crossed the Alps at twenty-six, but seldom, in the long perverse history of war, had a young commander been expected to achieve so much with so little.

Gordon at once reviewed his doubtful assets. He had five or six infantry regiments, according to the season, for at harvest time there were wholesale desertions. He had four field and two siege batteries, and the men were armed with smooth-bore muskets and a few Enfields. The uniform of the 'Ever Victorious Army' was green serge with green turbans, a uniform calculated to suggest they were foreigners and so much to be feared. Gordon,

[1] News of the disaster was carried mainly by runners on horseback, but in a very short space of time the Emperor, as well as the Treaty Port merchants, had heard the distressing news.

as commander, received £250 a month, his colonels were on a scale ranging from £75 to £100, and the majors, captains, and adjutants on a corresponding scale. His officers were a mixed bag of foreigners, brave but quarrelsome, most of whom drank and whored to excess. The privates, all Chinese, received £4 10s. a month. No one, of course, paid any taxes.

The difficulty was that under Burgevine the men had not been paid at all for months on end. Loot, opium, gold, girls, were the substitute rewards. On taking a city a scale of plunder would be drawn up and the pirates were supposed to abide by its decrees. This had undermined all discipline. A swarm of receivers followed the Army to buy the loot at very economic prices from the soldiers. The privates all smoked opium, if they could get it, and drank brandy if it was available. This led to fantastic feats both of insubordination and valour.[1]

The officers were not much better than the men. Germans, Americans, Scandinavians, Frenchmen, and Spaniards were among their number and, on storming a town or village, their first concern was to round up the young concubines of the rebel leaders who would then be favoured with the attentions of their new lords.[2]

It is perhaps characteristic of love in China at this time that the concubines do not seem to have been unduly perturbed by their abrupt change of masters. Sometimes, of course, there was a tragedy. A young lieutenant opened a cupboard in the Summer Palace at the time of the sacking, and into his arms fell a young concubine of fifteen—dead. Her master had given her an overdose of opium and bound her in a shroud rather than let her fall into the hands of the foreigners. . . .

At first Gordon's men objected to their uniform because they

[1] Those who have not been lucky enough to see a man floating on the golden cloud produced by alcohol after opium have missed an amazing sight. Self-confidence is boosted to a point where danger is laughed at, and opposition swept aside.

[2] Perhaps this is accounted for by the school of love that at this time was accepted in China. The man did not love the girl in the Western sense. He was aroused, teased, and inflamed by her and the moment of consummation was, if possible, 'unbearably' prolonged. In the case of the Emperor the custom was to insert two young women at the foot of the Imperial couch who would make their way up, competing with each other, until the recumbent figure either rejected them both, chose one, or they were allowed to pursue their mission together.

said they were laughed at as 'imitation foreign devils', but when the 'Ever Victorious Army' became victorious in fact as well as in name they became proud of it and carried it with great insolence. Gordon started to feed and pay and discipline the men himself, modelling the routine on the British Army. At dawn a bugle woke this disreputable rabble and by sunrise they were—much to their surprise—sweating in square-drills and marches.

There were a thousand things to be seen to, and Gordon saw to them all himself. The little man with the cane who never seemed to tire was the dynamo that hammered this assembly of ruffians into an army. He came to terms with the Chinese Treasury, using much guile, patience, and politeness to achieve his aim— regular payments for his officers and men. With forthright pleading he persuaded the British authorities to allow more British officers, on whom Gordon could rely, to be seconded to his force. The British Government, with characteristic prudence, placed these officers on half-pay, but Gordon saw to it that they did not suffer financially.

He could not wholly suppress either opium or drink among his men, but he made it clear that a man who was drugged or drunk might be shot if it led to him deserting his duty. The threat was taken seriously and had a wholesome effect. His own officers still had a number of young women whom they changed constantly. Gordon could do little about this as long as it did not interfere with duty. The commander himself never had a woman in his quarters, though by Chinese tradition the youngest and most beautiful should first have passed through his hands. He was secretly revolted by the sexual greed of his officers, his own instinct being for the companionship of men, and that as a receiver of affection rather than as one who bestowed it. In the extraordinary circumstance in which he found himself Gordon's disinterest in women worked out as a positive advantage. He had a quick perception of men, he sympathized with their angers, their follies, and their foibles, but he was not himself subject to the same temptations as they were. Knowing that in some respects he was different from the men he commanded became a cult with him, a cult that revealed itself in a number of small ways: in his nightly praying in his tent and in his refusal to carry any arms except his cane, which became as much a symbol of authority as a field marshal's baton.

Gordon was not only concerned in reorganizing the rank and file of his army. He was an engineer and he devoted much time to the primitive mechanization of his force. He made mantlets[1] to protect his gunners, pontoon equipment, bamboo ladders—stronger than wood for they bent without breaking—planks for short tramways and transport, and a dozen other ingenious devices.

With such an army, and with a flotilla of gunboats and steamers, he was soon ready to take the field against the Tai-Pings, but there was one more small matter to attend to. He was a captain, wasn't he? Yet, he commanded an army. The Chinese obligingly made the young captain a mandarin with the Chinese rank of brigadier. Gordon, who was always forgetful about the trappings of power as opposed to its reality, only thought of this matter at the last moment. He had been too busy to realize the incongruity of his rank. But the Chinese, who were experts in assessing the realities of power themselves, began to realize that here was a young man who was about to achieve greatness, and who cared not at all for honours.

The pace of events had been tremendous. Gordon almost forgot to inform his parents of what was afoot. But not quite. On the 24th of March 1863, the day before formally taking command, he writes home trying to assuage the blow that he thinks his activities will represent in the mind of his father. Usually he wrote to his mother, keeping an eye open for his father's reactions, but this time there was so much explaining to be done that he tackles the General directly, and the way he does it throws brilliant light on Gordon and the hidebound old soldier whom he never ceased to respect and love.

'I am afraid you will be much vexed at my having taken command of the Sung-Kiang Force and that I am now a mandarin.[2]

---

[1] The materials from which Gordon made the protective covering for his men and armour varied very much. The Chinese had some chain armour which Gordon was to use extensively later in Africa. But mainly the mantlets were locally made of tough fibre which was effective against most of the rebel weapons.

[2] Typically Gordon never tells his father that he has gone through the ceremony in which the mandarin's robes were presented usually by a viceroy on the Emperor's behalf. The ritual included bowing the head to the ground three times

I have taken the step on consideration and I promise not to act rashly. I feel that anyone helping to put down this rebellion is fulfilling a humane task, and helping to open China to civilization. . . .'

The argument is cunningly contrived to enlist the sympathies of General Gordon. Why, if his son won, China might become Christian, almost British!

'Had I not accepted the command I think this force might have been disbanded and the rebellion, and all its horror, gone on for years. As soon as I can I will return home.'

Whether the old general had his defences penetrated by this remarkably astute letter we do not know, but his son turned at once to the formation of his overall strategy.

Up to now the Imperial Government could hardly be said to have formed a strategic policy at all, unless it were to drive the rebels into the sea. This conception involved driving them towards the coastal foreign settlements and was much resented by the foreigners. Apart from this the Imperialists relied on day-to-day tactical moves, the clearing of certain areas, especially the suburbs of Shanghai, and the retributive assault on certain towns and villages that had been disloyal.

These activities, in their total effect, were calculated to prolong the rebellion indefinitely.

Gordon thought the matter over in seclusion with his maps through one long week-end. Then he emerged, and those strangely brilliant blue eyes were inhumanly bright. He had made up his mind. He would ignore retaliations and local engagements, he would refuse to be led here and there by the whims of the rebel commanders. He would gather his reorganized and disciplined army together and strike directly at the roots of power that sustained this rebellion. He was, of course, as yet in no position to march against their capital, but he could strike blows that would put the rebels on the defensive—and warn them that a strong and implacable man was determined to bring about their downfall.

---

in recognition of absolute fidelity to the Emperor. Did Gordon do this? There is no record that I can find that would indicate that he did. Perhaps an exception was made for a foreigner, but the Chinese expected foreigners to conform to their courtesies. Gordon was secretive about certain aspects of his career, and this may have been one of those episodes which he preferred not to dwell on.

6

Gordon Strikes Terror

GORDON understood very well the secret of success in war. His nature and his grasp of strategy and tactics both drove him into being an offensive commander constantly using surprise as his ally. He had made up his mind that the policy of 'containing' the rebellion was hopeless. To the rebels it seemed like compromise and toleration. Big areas were being left to them without dispute. These areas, of course, were indoctrinated with the perverse Christianity which the rebels had developed, and a cardinal political belief was hatred of the Manchu Dynasty and their 'Imperial imps'. The longer the rebels held their territory without being attacked, the more difficult would they be to dislodge.

Gordon saw that, in one way, the rebels were playing into his hands. The Manchus might be disliked by the majority of the people—they were arrogant, arbitrary, and alien. But the rebel Wangs—their headmen or kings—were even more detested. They knew no language but terror. They butchered and raped and looted wherever they went. They were almost inconceivably cruel. While observing their pagan version of Christianity with meticulous care, they behaved as if they were servants of the devil. Gordon noted this and decided to take advantage of it. He determined to show the utmost resolution and strength in battle, combined with the greatest clemency to prisoners and civilians. This, of course, was a new policy in China, but we shall see the rewards it brought.

When Gordon pored over his maps for hours on end[1] he could carry with him in his mind's eye the whole vast battlefield. He decided to strike where he was least expected—and to keep on striking. This policy he combined with plans to make his river craft play a part in operations. The rebels, much to their surprise, were to be subjected to amphibious attack. Gordon then improved the protection of his armour, making mantlets now of wood and even of iron. He always had the engineer's interest in mechanical warfare and one feels that, had he lived later, he would have been one of the very first tank-men. As it was, the mobility and striking force of his army was greatly increased by every kind of ingenious device: protective mantlets, trolleys, quickly laid rails, and every type of effective storming equipment.

On every side Gordon had to resist pressure to march immediately to avenge the defeat of Taitsan. The fact that Europeans had been captured and beheaded as well as the loss of two of the heaviest guns called, the critics said, for prompt retaliation. This was just what Gordon was trying to avoid. He would be expected in Taitsan. The rebel leaders were waiting for him to return. He must return, they thought, to save face. But he did not do so. Instead, he struck, with great rapidity and force, at Fushan and Chanzu.

Gordon had a double motive in directing his first attack in this way. Both Fushan and Chanzu commanded stretches of the Yangtze and both offered opportunities for amphibious warfare. Fushan was a rebel city, the former haunt of pirates, but there was an Imperialist force camped nearby under cover of which Gordon could start his operations. If he could recapture Fushan he could relieve Chanzu, whose loyal garrison were very hard pressed and who had had a recent history that gives a key to the fluctuations of loyalty and the fortunes of war in China. It is Mr Holmes the observant missionary to whom again we are indebted for a note on Chanzu:

'The garrison of Chanzu itself has a curious story to tell. They had all been rebels but had suddenly transferred their town and allegiance to the Emperor. Their chief Luo-Kue Chung

---

[1] Although Gordon could not always remember faces, he was able to carry minute topographical details in his head with complete accuracy.

had persuaded them to shave their heads and declare their allegiance to the Imperial Government earlier in the year and this they had done in conjunction with the Government of Fushan. To their dismay the Faithful King came down upon them with a large force—which included the two thirty-two-pounders captured at Taitsan—and stormed Fushan, which he retained in a grip of terror. The rebels tried to frighten the Chanzu garrison into surrender by sending them an envoy bearing the heads of three of the European officers killed and decapitated at Taitsan. But the rebels, taking counsel among themselves, decided that, if they capitulated, in spite of promises, because of their "treachery" they would receive no mercy. They decided to hold out, which they did with great courage and endurance.'

It takes little imagination to picture the relief of these doomed men when they heard that Gordon was attacking Fushan. They had no doubt that, once successful, he would relieve them, and they heard news of his progress with anxious delight.

On the 3rd of April we find Gordon on one of his two river-steamers sitting at a table near the prow where the wind was coolest, poring over his maps and giving last-minute instructions to his officers. On the two steamers were about a thousand men and these included two hundred of his artillery in which he took great pride for he had practised them in range-finding and fire concentration for weeks. It is typical of Gordon that his victories, which appear effortless, were usually preceded by hard work and much concentrated study.

He knew every street and bund and wall of Fushan before he went into the attack.

Gordon called his officers together and then, as they steamed up the Yangtze estuary towards Fushan, he gave his final orders. He pointed to a large-scale map he had himself drawn of Fushan.

'There.' The slim, white hand guided a pencil. 'There are the ruins caused by the previous attacks. They even penetrate the city and should afford fine cover for our guns. I want the thirty-two-pounder and the four twelve-pounder howitzers taken there as quickly and as secretly as possible. We attack at dawn. While it is still dusk the guns should be in position. There are two major stockades. They must be breached by gunfire before any infantry move in. . . .'

The young group of officers, listening, knew that here they had a leader who thought and planned—and cared. They made meticulous notes of their orders.

The creek that divided Gordon's army from the city itself was crossed by one of Gordon's most trusted officers, Captain Belcher, a gallant officer who used two boats for the purpose.

The rebels rushed heavy reinforcements from Chanzu and Gordon had to call off his operations for the day.

Gordon concealed from his officers the bitter disappointment he felt that his plan to storm Fuchan in a day had apparently failed.

Tired to the point of exhaustion, his overworked imagination that night painted for him a black picture. Why had he under-estimated the recuperative power of the rebels and their tenacity? Was he absurdly optimistic? Was he asking too much of his men? Had he failed in proper preparation? As he sought a few hours of fitful sleep nightmares haunted him. The rebels would win. Their leader would demand Gordon's head on a charger. The Manchu Dynasty would tumble into disruption and chaos.

The brandy he took gave him no comfort. But when he woke at dawn the first messenger that awaited him brought a message from spies who reported that the rebels were pulling out. They had suffered greater losses than they had ever received. They had hung on stubbornly until nightfall, not to strengthen resistance but to facilitate their withdrawal under cover of darkness. It was one of those lightning changes of fortune with which Gordon was to become familiar in the months ahead. The Chinese kaleidoscope was doing its conjuring trick of a quick and total change.

Gordon's mercurial spirits rose. Why had he doubted? His star was rising. Only he could do this thing. It was a mission and he intended it to be a mission of success. The optimism that their commander radiated infected his officers and men. From now on the 'Ever Victorious Army' marched with a high morale.

Within twelve hours Fushan was captured. There was no resisting Gordon's carefully planned tactics. His gunners, protected as he had foreseen by the scattered ruins which were massive and widely spread, opened up a devastating fire. The ramparts crumbled and confusion seized the city.

The local Wang, a man of thirty-five, came out to present gifts to Gordon: a gold drinking-cup, an antelope, and two virgins, children not more than twelve years old and 'very smooth and soft'.

'He chin-chinned with great rapidity, apparently very relieved that it was all over. I told him I could not take the gifts as it was not customary in our country. He appeared very surprised, but relieved when I told him that his life would be spared and that, after they had been vetted, his troops might be allowed to join my forces. . . .'

Gordon's victory enabled him to relieve Chanzu at once, and this he did with a large number of Imperial troops supporting his 'Ever Victorious Army' which was at last beginning to live up to its name. Gordon, leaving a garrison of three hundred men at Fushan, returned to his headquarters at Sung-Kiang to plan a further campaign.

He received a letter expressing the Emperor's warmest congratulations from Li-Hung-Chang, his immediate superior and a mandarin of the Yellow Button.

Burgevine, the sinister American with his bloated, cunning features and unwieldy frame, had not lost hope of ousting Gordon from his command and being reinstated. He knew that in China all things are possible, but he realized that with the news of Gordon's victories coming in he would have to work fast. He did. He was able to start two rumours that eventually fed the radical press at home and gave Gordon the greatest trouble. The first was that his losses had been far greater than had ever been admitted, and this rumour, false in itself, was bolstered by one under-estimation by Gordon which was corrected two days later. The second slander was that Gordon was concurring in traditional Chinese torture. In fact the whole of Gordon's plan for the reconquest of rebel China was based on conquest plus conversion. But he was unable to restrain occasional acts of savagery. In Fushan one rebel commander was secretly flayed alive after Gordon had returned to his headquarters and Burgevine—who, himself, was completely ruthless—worked this up in a story of Gordon atrocities for an eager audience in London.

It seems incredible now that Burgevine should very nearly have ousted Gordon, even after the Fushan victory. That he was able to come very near to doing so was due to the fact that the American Minister warmly supported him, and Sir Frederick Bruce, the British Ambassador, appears to have taken more interest in Burgevine than he did in Gordon. However, those who were nearer events, those who had to fight this vast guerilla war, were determined to retain Gordon. Li wrote to Prince Kung 'Gordon is our man, and we can have no other.' This unusual frankness on the part of the man to whom the Emperor was looking for results settled the matter. Burgevine left Shanghai in disgust, muttering dark curses against all and sundry and embarking on a monumental drinking-bout. But Burgevine was too ambitious to be consoled for ever with alcohol. He turned later to treachery, as we shall see.

Gordon spent a month in carefully correcting weaknesses that the troops had revealed in their operations on Fushan and Chanzu. He had the greatest difficulty in procuring for them regular payment: in the end, through the good offices of an urbane and honest Treasury official named Kah, he accomplished this. The young commander had banners made for his regiments on the English model. They were cherished and served as a rallying-point in battle. No banner of the 'Ever Victorious Army' was ever captured.

Gordon disciplined his men and his officers by a graded system of punishment for offences, as well as better conditions of service. These included, in the case of officers, the fear of instant dismissal by their commanding officer. Gordon did not believe in appeals from his judgment.

Gordon was ready now to march on Quinsan which held a strategic position in relation both to Soochow and Taitsan, but was diverted by a message he received from Li. Gordon was returning to his tent at dusk when the messenger arrived. He read the hastily written letter quickly.

'We received proposals of surrender from Taitsan and accordingly sent a force to parley and take over. During the talks our force was treacherously attacked and slaughtered during the dark hours, as they were sleeping. . . .'

Gordon made up his mind in an instant. He had refused to walk into the trap of attacking Taitsan to save face and avenge Captain Holland's defeat, but treachery of this kind merited instant retribution.

Taitsan had a very strong garrison, who felt themselves triumphantly immune from retaliation. They numbered over ten thousand men. Gordon had but three thousand men at most, but they were highly organized. Protective mantlets heavily made of iron and wood protected his gunners. Gordon used two gunboats in this manœuvre with the greatest effect, concentrating on the rebel arsenal which was reduced to ashes after a series of deafening explosions that had their effect in lowering rebel morale —the spirits were unfriendly to the defenders, it was said. Gordon also used, for the first time in China, the technique of firing over the heads of his men, protecting them by the barrage at the same time that he reduced the enemy ramparts.

Gordon lost nearly 10 per cent of his men, but the rebel losses were fearsome. In the end, after many had fled, not more than three hundred troops, including two Wangs, were left alive to capitulate. It was the first major victory. Suddenly China awoke one morning to the previously incredible thought that this terrifying rebellion might be smashed within a year.

The victory was marred by one incident. Seven of the prisoners taken, were, without Gordon's knowledge, condemned by the Imperial commander to slow and ignominious death. They were exhibited in chains for two days without water or food, made to crawl on their knees a mile to the place of execution, and there flayed alive with spears piercing their body in various places. They took a long time to die. An Imperialist chronicler reported that four of the victims were still 'wriggling' the next morning. This, of course, was something which Gordon's enemies at home and in China could seize on, but Gordon did not remain silent.

In a letter to the *Shanghai Shipping News* dated the 15th of June 1863 he says:

'I am of the belief that the soldiers of this force are as merciful

Gordon as a mandarin and servant
of the Chinese Empire

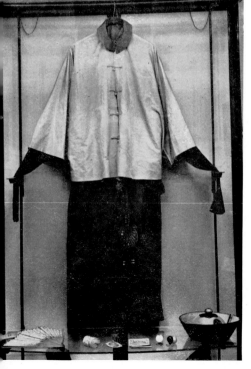

The yellow jacket (Chinese
mandarin) worn by General
Gordon

Gordon as Governor-General of the Sudan, his uniform a strange
combination of Ottoman and British styles

as any Christian force would be. Over seven hundred men taken prisoner in the recent operation are now in our employ. Over fifteen hundred rebels were killed by the populace in their retreat from Quinsan. If "Observer", "Eye-Witness", etc., think that the people like their rebel masters, let them come here and see for themselves. . . .'

This open invitation was not accepted by the parties concerned. The truth is, of course, that Gordon was not able to control the Imperial forces, and only with difficulty at times could he restrain the 'Ever Victorious Army' from taking 'customary steps'. In flaying alive and crucifying only seven of the Quinsan garrison the Chinese had acted with what they regarded as great forbearance. 'We were if anything too clement,' wrote General Li.

Gordon hardly paused in his operations before returning to invest Quinsan, his original objective before he was diverted to Taitsan.

A chain of creeks opening at times into small lakes led to the city, and the little steamer, the *Hyson*, was manned with guns protected with mantlets to play its part in the operation. Nearly fifty smaller gunboats were mobilized and these, all flying the Imperial banner and the banners of the 'Ever Victorious Army', gave Gordon a powerful little fleet which he used to the utmost advantage both in the attack on Quinsan and in harassing the rebels when in their hundreds they fled the city. Having but one road to take, and this commanded by his water-borne artillery terror, a sense of calamity seized the rebels. They were never safe from their ingenious and implacable pursuer.

Gordon writes at this time: 'The horror of the rebels at the steamer is very great. When she whistles they cannot make it out and panic seizes them. . . .'

Gordon was never free of trouble even in his hours of victory. The captured towns had to be garrisoned and held. Less and less were the troops able to return to the amenities of Sung-Kiang— the girls, the opium, the cheap alcohol, and—perhaps most important of all—the established receivers to whom they could dispose of their loot. Gordon had spies among his men—he needed them. 'How else,' he said, 'can I discover what is going

E

on?'[1]—and one of these brought him a document inciting his troops to mutiny against the stern discipline of their commander and to ask for the reinstatement of Burgevine.

Gordon acted instantly. Parading his whole army he asked for the names of the writers. If he were not told he said one in five would be shot. This evoked loud groans among the non-commissioned officers. Gordon had the loudest groaner shot out of hand. It was enough. The mutiny was broken. As so often, Gordon was lucky. The shot man turned out to be the leader of the abortive coup.

Gordon went to rest that night feeling that, for the moment, a great danger had past. He stripped off his uniform, said his prayers, took his large swig of brandy, and then wrote to his mother:

'I am now a Tsung Ping, a mandarin of the second class. You may rest assured [this apparently in reply to an agitated query from his father] that I never appear in Chinese robes, even at ceremonies. The mandarins are most civil these days, and at last we have the rebels on the run. It is the beginning of the end. I am showered with honours and presents, but I do not care over much about that; I am sure I was right to take over this command. You would agree if you could see the character of the rebels.'

Having made his peace with his Maker, his mother and father, within minutes this extraordinary man was again enjoying his peaceful sleep, undisturbed by the nightmares that might well have assailed him.

He had that very British approach to problems that could be summed up by saying: 'I do my best. Nothing else matters.' But there was one image that haunted Gordon, the image of Burgevine. In spite of the plotting that Gordon knew Burgevine constantly indulged in, Gordon had a liking for this gangster. He was virile, rude, intensely masculine. He could and did deflower six virgins in a night. He drank a bottle of rice wine as if it were water. He had no scruples. For Gordon, Burgevine was the opposite of everything that he felt in his own nature. At a time when Burgevine

---

[1] Gordon in China and later in the Sudan relied greatly on espionage, which he regarded as the essential handmaiden of military operations and government.

was to perpetrate his greatest deceit and treachery by selling himself to the enemy, Gordon himself was scheming to get him back into the fold so that he and his followers would strengthen the 'Ever Victorious Army', and Gordon would have at his side the man for whom he nurtured a secret tenderness.[1]

[1] The extraordinary solicitation of Gordon for Burgevine, revealed in innumerable letters, even when it was obvious that the American was a worthless renegade, appears to be explicable only by the assumption that Burgevine fascinated Gordon. It is true that Burgevine had a following of gangsters that might, at certain times, be important in the balance of power between the Imperialists and the rebels, but, in such cases where his affections were not aroused, Gordon could be ruthless.

7

Burgevine Intrigues

IT IS not easy in these more conventional days to understand, far less appreciate, the figure and character of Burgevine. Burgevine was a southerner and a mercenary. He was in China for the money, and because he liked the cheap drink and the women. It was a man's life, he frequently said, where strength and cunning paid off. If he could have ousted Gordon from his command by underground intrigue, that was all part of the game. He knew that Gordon had a weakness for him and suspected that, if he was ever in great danger, Gordon would intervene on his behalf. He was right in thinking this. Burgevine sometimes treated Gordon with contempt, but more often he 'got round him' by being gay and incorrigibly charming. Then all his sins were forgiven, and he would bask for a time in Gordon's favour.

But Burgevine was so angered by the defeat of his plots to get reinstated—in any capacity—that he now decided on a serious step. He decided to sell himself to the rebels. This was a dangerous move. It would mean that he was in the hands of the rebel commanders. He managed, however, to bring with him three hundred men of his own kind: drinkers, whorers, and adventurers, who formed a tough and ruthless little fighting force.

The investment and capture of Soochow was the next objective on the list of both Gordon and the Imperialists and, in carrying out his grand design for the capture of this most important city, Gordon was greatly helped by the fact that the city was the central intersection of a great many fine canals and lakes, making a highly developed attack by water and by land possible.

Gordon heard the news of Burgevine's treachery with despair and grief. But in all the letters he wrote on the matter there is hardly a word of reproach. His whole objective was to win Burgevine back. It was not easy. Burgevine himself was in danger. He had not carried out all his promises to the rebels and some of his followers had deserted the rebel cause and returned to the Imperialists, or left China.

But Gordon was prepared to go to any lengths to win back Burgevine. On the 18th of October 1863 he even wrote a long letter from the Stockades, Patachow, addressed to the Chung Wang and Moh Wang asking them to release their European mercenaries on the ground that they could no longer rely on them and that, if they were ever tortured or put to death, the Wangs would be storing up trouble for themselves in the future. It is clear that Gordon was haunted by the fear of losing Burgevine for ever.

Unexpectedly Gordon's letter met with success. The Wangs decided after many parleys to allow their Europeans to go free. Burgevine took advantage of this, while they still were so minded, and turned up with thirty of his gangsters at Gordon's camp.

Gordon, at his stiffest and most uncompromising, lectured Burgevine on loyalty and the ethics of the soldier. Burgevine laughed at him. 'That's all very well for you, Kernel,' he said (he called Gordon 'Kernel' much to Gordon's disgust), 'but for me *no*. I'm here for the pickings and the life. I like the life. Have I showed you Yok Lin? The longest legs in China. But seriously, Kernel, you and I could do ourselves a lot of good right now . . .'

'What is it you are suggesting?'

'You and I, Kernel, take the lot. Your lot and my men join up and we take China. Set up in Nanking if you like. Lords of the Yangtze. You can be emperor. I'll be the Na Wang, your chief man. Soon we'll have them all licking our boots. Your ambassador, my minister. The Anglo-American entente. Peace, progress, and the rule of law, Kernel. And for you and me all the gold and girls in China. Now I could not do this without you.

You've got something—goodness perhaps, reputation. But you would never do it without me. You haven't the unconventional approach. You haven't the idea in your mind. We're made for each other, Kernel. What about it?'

When Gordon heard this startling proposal he was not immediately horrified, except at the way in which it attracted him. He and Burgevine could do this thing. He didn't want to be a British officer, really,[1] with all the restrictions that implied. This life would give him fame, riches, and power. It was with surprise that he heard himself turn on Burgevine and say: 'You had better go. What you suggest is unpardonable. I tried to save you for something better than that. . . .'

But Burgevine only laughed. 'Well, think it over, Kernel,' he said, and was gone.

Gordon felt the emptiness of his tent without the hulking intensely living figure of Burgevine. He might smell of alcohol and women but he smelt too of life, abounding life, lived to the full and recklessly. Gordon closed the sheets of his tent and sank to his knees, the tears streaming down his face, for one of those talks with his Maker that were a feature of his life. On the whole, God and Gordon got on very well. Gordon was completely candid in prayer. It was the confessional without a priest. And that night Gordon stripped himself of his legend.

'I am not brave, and I love power and pomp. I am a fraud. I disdain the gifts of victory because I am afraid to take them. I pretend to be brave when inwardly I tremble. And I am not clean and pure in thought.'[2]

Having said all this, and come face to face with himself as he really was, Gordon began to recover his confidence. In a very real way he felt his prayer for strength answered. Next day he stepped into the early-morning sunshine without a doubt in the world. Brisk and alert he was the Gordon of legend again, the Gordon who, armed with his cane alone, would gently lead a

---

[1] Throughout his entire career Gordon, from time to time, got very tired of Gordon, the British legend. This boredom with his own image grew as the image itself grew greater.

[2] No one can say for certain what form Gordon's self-castigation took, but I feel that an attempt should be made to recreate these important incidents in Gordon's personal struggle with himself.

fearful young officer into the hottest part of an engagement and say: 'There, you see. It's not so bad, after all. . . .'

Gordon at these times of self-examination and personal crisis was completely honest with himself. He thought that sexual tendencies were evil—a secret shame in the Victorian language of the day. He knew that he had a tendency to play up to the legend of Gordon, which, while still so young, he had created. And he knew that his austerity was clung to because he feared indulging in a longing for wealth, luxury, and unbridled power. Because he saw this clearly in his moments of self-revelation he was able to win these spiritual battles, but they cost him more in anguish than his campaigns ever did. His campaigns were for him the high skirmish of life itself. He understood and mastered them, but his own spirit and cravings were more difficult to regulate. His private torment he kept to himself. It was a matter between Gordon and God, and it seems that Gordon's God understood this strange man and helped him, so that in spite of moments of black anger and hopelessness he always rose above his difficulties to carry on with whatever task he had in hand.

Gordon had schooled himself to contain the frustration and annoyance which Chinese prevarication and cunning often aroused in him, but now one breach of faith, so awful in its nature and consequences, was to anger him almost beyond endurance.

The investment of Soochow was a major undertaking and the 'Ever Victorious Army' under Gordon played an important part in it, though the number of Imperial troops under direct Chinese command was far greater. However, Gordon on military matters had come to an understanding with the Imperial High Command. They still indulged in tactical operations without consulting Gordon—often with disastrous results—but on major strategy there was broad agreement.

Soochow was to be taken after a planned, slow, deliberate encirclement, cutting off the city from all supplies and thus imposing military strangulation. It was a strategy that ensured ultimate success with the minimum of loss. This was always Gordon's underlying objective. Then, as the great squeeze began to tighten, it was learned that there was disagreement among the Wangs within the besieged city. Moh Wang, a Chinese of great stature and courage, was for defending the city at all cost. He was as brave as a lion and saw clearly that if Soochow went the road lay open to Nanking and the ultimate ruin of the rebel cause. Suspicious of the loyalty of his fellow Wangs, Moh Wang called them into council when he told them that this was a fight to the finish. The other Wangs were about to accept this terrifying decision when Kong Wang suddenly drew his dagger and stabbed Moh Wang three times through the heart, so that he died at once. Now the Wangs were free to do what they wanted to do, that is to negotiate. At this point Governor Li, suspecting that the Wangs would not accept his assurances of safe conduct, persuaded Gordon to take over the negotiations. Gordon asked the Governor: 'Do you really intend to spare the lives of these men?' Li replied smoothly: 'Certainly, that is our intention.' On this basis Gordon negotiated the capitulation of the city.

The taking of a city as big as Soochow led to the greatest chaos in the last hours before surrender, and Gordon at one point found himself cut off from his men and a prisoner of the rebels. He might have expected death or torture, but neither came his way, for the reputation of Gordon had spread not only to the Imperial Court and to the foreign merchants but also to the rebel commanders. They understood him to be brave, merciful, and a man of his word. Perhaps now he could procure a pardon for them and assuage the Imperial wrath. Had they known that, at that very moment, the Wangs were one and all being crucified by the Imperial troops, there is little doubt that Gordon would have died there and then. As it was he was released with a prayer that he would help them if he could.

It was not many hours before Gordon discovered the truth. He was black with anger. He had been used by Li who had never had any intention of sparing the Wangs. General Ching also had been a party to the deception. Gordon despatched rockets to all and sundry, including General Brown in Shanghai. He had been grossly deceived. He had been made a tool of dishonour. He resigned his command and asked to leave for Britain at once.

These outbursts of righteous wrath were received with calmness by the authorities, both British and Chinese. Yes, of course Gordon had been made use of. That was perhaps inevitable, but the putting to death of the Wangs was not more than they deserved. It was the custom, and in China what was customary was lawful and proper.

The murder of the Wangs had fierce repercussions. Here was something which Gordon's enemies could exploit, and exploit it they did. Gordon was at the bar of world opinion, but he did not this time strive to defend himself. Instead, after cooling down, he realized that were he to quit now it might be taken as a signal for this awful rebellion that was tottering to stand again and bring more terror and unhappiness to millions of Chinese. Gordon withdrew his resignation and resumed work. He even made it up with Li-Hung-Chang.

In coming to this decision Gordon was prompted by the generous thanks of the Emperor who sent him the red jacket and 10,000 taels in cash as well as a letter of thanks in gold ink. Gordon kept the letter and the red jacket, but returned the money. The foreigners in the Treaty Ports also spoke of him in terms that made it difficult for him to give up. Wrote a Mr Hart: 'The destiny of China, at this moment, is in the hands of Charles Gordon.'

So Gordon stayed and fought. But indeed the main fighting for the 'Ever Victorious Army' was over. Whereas only a few months before the rebel cause had been dominant, and the people had flocked to the standards of the Heavenly King, now the Imperial writ began again to be respected. As soon as it was clear that the Manchus were to retain power every governor in China wished to dissociate himself from the rebel cause and declare his unswerving allegiance to the Emperor.

Quickly, with growing confidence and in greater numbers, the Imperialists advanced on the last stronghold of the rebel king, the fortress and palace of Nanking where for years the 'brother of God', the Heavenly King, had reigned in undisputed sovereignty.

As the Imperial forces came ever closer and the deserters from the rebel ranks increased alarmingly, some of his closest supporters whispered in the ear of Hang-Tsue-Chuen that he should flee while there was yet time. He could melt back into the millions of China from whence he had come. He had many friends, this fearsome fanatic, and they would hide him.

But the rebel king was now gripped with a megalomania that knew no reason. Was he not the Lord of Life, the brother of God, the master of the mountains and the valleys? And the rebel court, from long habit, sank to its knees and assured him that he was, indeed, all these things.

So life went on in the jade bedroom and in the marble audience-hall as it had done for many years. The ceremonies were held, the prayers were said, and the Heavenly King was worshipped. Then one morning a messenger came saying that the Imperialists were within striking distance of the city; and there was none to resist them. The dreams of the Heavenly King were shattered at last. But he was no coward. He refused to listen to any counsel of despair. Quietly he prepared his ten wives and himself for death.

At first the Heavenly King thought that his wives should be sewn up in silken bags and beaten to death without spilling blood, for was not that the manner in which Eastern princesses were executed? But the chief wife interceded saying that this would cause unnecessary suffering. The King nodded. He was mad, now, perhaps, but he was compassionate. One by one the wives were executed with a sharp and shining sword so that one stroke was sufficient to cut right through each soft little neck.

Then Hang-Tsue-Chuen sat down before his own altar and with his gold knife he cut an artery in his wrist and in his throat. As the Imperialists stormed into the city he sat there, immobile. Then he slumped into a coma and soon was dead, a sacrifice to his own ambition.

For a time the turbulence that had stricken China was stilled. And no one had done more to bring this about than the odd little British commander who was now a mandarin and whose name had become a legend among foreigners and Chinese alike.

8

Victory

T H E fall of Nanking, which meant the end of the rebellion, was preceded by the last important engagements in which Gordon took part. He himself led an attack on Kintang and was shot in the leg while doing so. The Chinese, usually jealous and secretive, were deeply moved by the fact that they had nearly lost their friend and most energetic commander. Even the Emperor, who habitually remained suitably detached from the fluctuations of mortal warfare, wrote to Li-Hung-Chang:

'Li-Hung-Chang reports that Gordon, some time since, started from Liyang to attack Kintang and while doing so was wounded in the leg. This was the result of his excessive valour, energy, and disregard of personal safety. Li-Hung-Chang is to persuade Gordon to rest until he recovers, and is to visit him daily till he does so. Respect this!'

One doubts whether any accolade ever bestowed by the Chinese on a foreigner can have been more sincere or more revealing of the real Chinese feelings than this note by the Son of Heaven to his governor. It even looks as if Gordon had captured a place in the affections of the Emperor, though of course this could not be admitted.

Gordon was shocked to hear that General Ching, one of the few honest and brave Chinese commanders, had died of a wound in the head. General Ching met his death with composure, donning, at the last moment, the yellow jacket, bowing towards the

75

Imperial Palace in Pekin, and then meeting his end with the fortitude of his race. Gordon wept when he heard the news. When he was deeply moved he was always capable of tears and was unable to hold them back.

The last major engagement that Gordon took part in was the capture of Chanchu-fu. Then out of the blue something happened that brought the intrigues and contortions of politics in London right out to China. The British Government abruptly withdrew permission for its officers to enlist in or serve with the 'Ever Victorious Army'. The step was taken without consulting Gordon. It was a stunning step to take without any notice, but, in fact, Gordon's work was done. He himself, on his own initiative, now disbanded the 'Ever Victorious Army'. His view was that, with their foreign officers, they had no place in a China to which peace was being rapidly restored.

The letters of 'Eye-witness', 'Justice', etc., and the radical press at home, had never ceased to attack Gordon, and it was no doubt the culminating effect of this denigration that led to the order that no more officers were to be enlisted in Gordon's force and to withdraw those who were serving. Though Gordon must have resented the manner in which this decisive step was taken, he made no complaint. His reply was the disbandment of his command.

Gordon's ideas on what should be done in China were far ahead of his times. His underlying belief was that China was for the Chinese, and he now devoted himself to ensuring that Nanking was really about to fall to the Imperial forces and to giving advice to the Chinese commanders to ensure that this would happen. As we know, the tremendous news that the city had fallen and that the Heavenly King had been found dead with his wives in the Porcelain Tower came earlier than even the most sanguine expected. It was the signal for some unique honours offered to Gordon. The British Government might insist that they had hardly heard of him, but China, in the person of its Emperor, was grateful, so grateful that Gordon, at his head-quarters—he had just returned from a visit to Nanking—awoke on the 14th of June 1864—it was a Saturday and Gordon had slept late—to see an extraordinary concourse of men and banners congregated round his tent.

The assembly had been there some time but had let him sleep on, for in China it was not polite to wake sleeping friends, lest the spirits that had roamed during the night might not have time to return to their habitat as they would do when waking slowly and naturally.

Seated in the middle of the concourse of mandarins and their followers was Li, and he rose as Gordon emerged, smiling.

Li shook hands with Gordon in the European manner, then hugged him. Then he stood and read the Emperor's proclamation which was carried on a golden platter by two attendants.

'We are charged with bringing you a message from the Throne[1] to say that your great services to China are remembered by us and that we are grateful. You are made Ti-Tu [the highest rank in the Chinese Army], are hereby presented with the yellow jacket to replace the red jacket you have already received, you shall also receive the feather of a mandarin for your hat, and our Order, the Star of China. In addition General Li has been instructed to present to you a monetary gift in token of our regard. We have also written to your Ambassador asking him to inform our friend the gracious Queen of England of your outstanding services to us.

'Respect this.'

Gordon was overcome by the magnificence and generosity of these words. In instinctive return he bowed three times in the Chinese manner, feeling that any more British expressions of thanks would be quite inadequate. There and then, in the hot sun of a Chinese summer morning—the eleventh of the fifth moon of the third year of Tung-che—Gordon took the seat that Li had sat in and was invested with his honours. The yellow jacket, his cone-shaped mandarin's hat, the Star of China in gold and diamonds was pinned to his breast. Then Li and all the mandarins, in a spontaneous expression of their feelings such as certainly had never been accorded to a foreigner in China before, sank to their knees and touched the earth three times with their foreheads. It was a unique and touching occasion.

Now the Emperor, knowing Gordon by this time, slipped

[1] It is clear that the Emperor took the greatest personal interest in Gordon and his achievements. As a rule all routine administrative matters were dealt with by the Nei-Ko, or Cabinet, according to the precepts laid down in the Ta-Ts'ing-Huei-Tien, a compendium of law and moral precepts.

in the monetary reward quietly at the end of his proclamation, but Gordon steadfastly declined it. It amounted to some £20,000, but neither Li nor anyone could persuade this obstinate British officer to take what they regarded as his just reward.

On the 12th of July 1864 Sir Frederick Bruce wrote to Earl Russell as follows:

'I enclose the translation of a despatch from the Emperor's Minister, Prince Kung, concerning the decree published by His Imperial Majesty acknowledging the services of Lieutenant-General Gordon, Royal Engineers, and requesting that Her Majesty's Government should be pleased to recognize them.

'Colonel Gordon deserves well of Her Majesty's favour for, apart from his exceptional skill and courage in helping to suppress the rebellion, he has by his disinterestedness elevated our national character in the eyes of China. . . .'

The British Government were not unduly moved by this appeal. They made Gordon a full colonel, and some time later made him a Companion of the Order of the Bath.

But if the British Government, eight thousand miles from the impact of the terror of the rebellion, were cautious in their praise, the merchants of Shanghai, representing all the great British trading houses in China, had no doubt to whom they owed their security, and indeed their continued existence.

In November, just before his departure, Gordon received their formal thanks. In a letter they wrote:

'On the eve of your departure for your native land, we, the undersigned, mostly of your own nationality but also representing other nationalities here, wish to express to you our earnest wish for a happy and safe voyage and a return to your friends and the land of your birth.

'You have done more than any other man, by your courage, energy and selflessness to remove many of the prejudices that warp[1] the Chinese mind in respect of foreigners, and have established a relationship unique in our experience. Once more wishing you a safe journey and a long and successful career.'

---

[1] Chinese readers are asked to bear in mind that 'warped' was one of the least offensive adjectives used by the British at this time to describe those who disagreed with them!

Gordon replied, on the 25th of November 1864, briefly:

'Gentlemen,

'I have the honour to acknowledge receipt of your handsome
letter and to express the satisfaction I feel at the honourable
mention you have made of my services to China.

'I will always be deeply impressed with the honour you have
paid me.

'I have the honour to be, Gentlemen,

Yours obediently,
C. G. Gordon.'

And that was that.

There is one question that is always asked and has not,
perhaps, been adequately answered. How did he do it? How did
this junior British officer achieve the seemingly impossible? How
was Gordon able, within eighteen months, to smash one of the
most formidable, dangerous, and extensive revolts that China
had ever witnessed?

Briefly the answer might be that Britain, whose star was now
in the ascendant, had the right man in the right place at the right
time; but, of course, the real answer is more complicated, com-
prising, as it does, all the factors, some personal, others historical,
that made it possible for Gordon to achieve what he did.

First we must put the character of Gordon himself. Men,
friends and foes alike, recognized in him some rare quality. It
may have been goodness, but if it was it was not the goodness of
the saint. It was the goodness of a man sometimes troubled and
tormented, often tempted, whose simple faith made him strong,
compassionate, and unswerving. The Chinese are very good
judges of character. They do not ask that foreigners should fit
into a Chinese frame. Being intensely civilized in their assessments,
they are capable of seeing merit whatever form it takes. Gordon
was deeply appreciated not only by the Emperor but by every
Chinese of discernment he met.

Hand in hand with this man's character goes his personal
magnetism. Gordon made his own character, his magnetism was
a gift of God. There is no explaining this extraordinary quality.
We recognize it, but cannot define it. The odious, terrifying Hitler

had it. Lloyd George had it in Britain. Roosevelt had it in America, its magnetic force making his broken body unimportant. Men were attracted to Gordon individually and in a mass. He could implant the mark of his personality on any group. His men loved him though they feared him. His cane, the only weapon he carried, was talked about throughout China. It became the 'magic wand' of Chinese legend.

Then, added to these qualities of character and personal magnetism, were his gifts as a soldier. Of course he was very young, but he was not inexperienced. The Crimea had been a hard, revealing school, educating Gordon in the horrors and realities of warfare. There the British troops were pitted against a determined courageous enemy. No one who has fought the Russians defending their own country has ever forgotten the experience.

He was much more experienced than his years of service would suggest. And then he was a born soldier as well as a trained 'sapper'. From the first he understood the essentials of strategy and tactics and his inventive, unconventional mind probed out after new methods of surprise and attack.

His strategy was combined of at least three major qualities. He never did what he was expected to do unless some overriding consideration made him do so. He was the master of surprise. He employed new techniques because he appreciated the effectiveness of novelty. Thus his 'creeping barrage', enabling his armour to protect his advancing troops at the same time that he was demolishing the enemy stockades, instead of separating these operations, took the Chinese off guard. The third and basic asset that Gordon always had was thorough preparation. He planned his battles in meticulous detail, so that the tactics fell into the pattern of the strategy and the strategy of each encounter fitted into the overall design—the utter defeat of the rebels in the shortest time with the minimum loss.

As well as these personal assets of brain and heart, Gordon was lucky in his era. At this time the Chinese attributed almost miraculous powers to Europeans. Many of them doubted whether the foreigners could be killed by mortal means. The red foreign soldier was greatly feared. Gordon, as we know, exploited this.

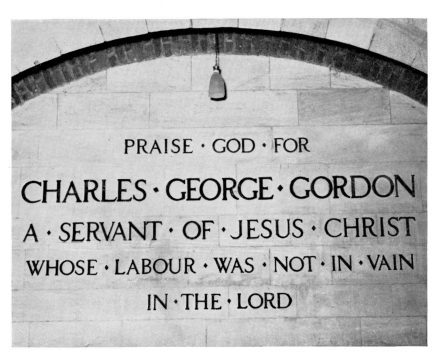

PRAISE · GOD · FOR

CHARLES · GEORGE · GORDON

A · SERVANT · OF · JESUS · CHRIST

WHOSE · LABOUR · WAS · NOT · IN · VAIN

IN · THE · LORD

The Church's view of Gordon; so different from Kitchener, who 'hated missionaries'. A Khartoum Cathedral inscription

Gordon's bed

Mail worn by Gordon's men

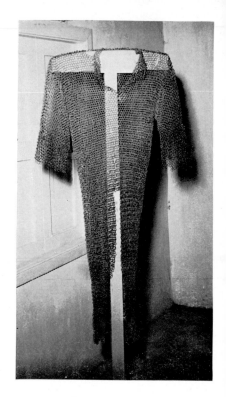

Gordon's prayer rug—identical with a Moslem rug except that it does not seem to have the design which may be pointed to Mecca

The uniform of the 'Ever Victorious Army' was a foreign uniform. Even their boots—when they could be persuaded to wear them—were designed to leave a foreign imprint.

Gordon was continuing his services to China as he received his manifold honours. He refused all invitations in Shanghai from the foreign communities and their embassies. He was busy until the last moment collaborating with Governor Li on a plan to train a Chinese élite corps to replace the 'Ever Victorious Army'. He made the most minute recommendations to the Chinese High Command for the reorganization of their army, including advice on regular payment, regimental organization, and welfare.

He spent his last weeks instructing the new Chinese Army and wrote home:

'I am getting on very well with my Chinese officers[1] and they make great progress knowing the manual, platoon, and gun drill already. . . .'

It is pleasant to be able to record that Gordon took the most meticulous care to reward the officers and men of the disbanded 'Ever Victorious Army'. He might refuse monetary rewards himself, but he did not expect others to do so. Each officer received a small fortune, and each man enough to set him up in some market-stall or smallholding. It is easy to believe that among the men of the 'Ever Victorious Army' Colonel Gordon would not be forgotten.

And Burgevine? He reverted to the rebels again, and later became a simple robber-chief until he met his death of a surfeit of women, rice wine, and disease. Burgevine was beyond redemption.

Gordon sailed for England but wrote, typically, to his mother: 'The individual is coming home, but does not wish it to be known, for it would be the signal for the disbanded to come to Southampton. The waits at Christmas are bad, but these others are worse. . . .'

This lonely, inhibited man just could not face a jovial hero's greeting at Southampton. He turned up, unannounced, at his father's house in London.

---

[1] Gordon took the trouble to learn some useful—and polite—phrases in Mandarin, speaking with the correct tone. He also mastered a large number of military terms and orders in Chinese.

F

'Chinese Gordon' had come home.

In a period of twenty months he had saved the Imperial Throne of China from what looked like certain doom, but he was glad to be back in his own cold country with its Christmas fog and sleet. The mandarin vanished, and Colonel Gordon, Royal Engineers, took his place.

Part Two

9

Gravesend Interlude

GORDON managed to slip into England avoiding both the Press—whom he profoundly distrusted—and the public, on his return from China. He turned up unannounced at his parents' house and to his father he told the tale of his eventful eighteen months of service in the 'Ever Victorious Army'. Even now, as a grown man of experience, he was never quite at home with the General. His father's views were so rigid, so conventional, and so strongly held that Gordon constantly found himself framing the story in a way that he thought would not arouse the old gentleman's disapproval.

The service in the ranks of the Chinese Emperor, his close friendship with many Chinese,[1] his affection for the Chinese people, his honours received from the Emperor himself, all these had to be skated over lest General Gordon should feel that his son had been guilty of 'antics' to please foreigners. It was best to concentrate on strategy and tactics. These interested his father intensely and, together, poring over maps to illustrate his points, the son probably got as near to his father as he was capable of getting. After all they were both soldiers, so they had what has always proved to be one of the closest ties binding two men.

While father and son conversed, bringing to life the battles of the 'Ever Victorious Army', the employment of amphibious methods against the surprised rebels, the revelation of Chinese

---

[1] Many of his Chinese friends wrote to him for years, and followed his career with interest.

cunning, cruelty and, on occasion, discernment and loyalty, Mrs Gordon quietly regarded them both. She was overjoyed to have her son back. He might easily have been killed in China. She had read in a letter to *The Times* that:

'Besides his favourite cane, he carried nothing except field-glasses. Gordon's quiet undress uniform without belts, buckles, or any weapon, contrasted strangely with the buccaneering, brigand-like costume of the American mercenaries, strapped, armed, and booted like theatrical banditti.'

Unarmed, relying on the almost mesmeric quality of his leadership, he had, somehow, come through, surviving the greatest dangers. It was, his mother thought, something to thank God for.

Mrs Gordon was an intelligent, intuitive person and the details of how the victories had been won left her puzzled and dissatisfied. What she wanted to know was the kind of life her son had been leading, who his friends had been, what the Emperor had thought of him—and what the mandarin 'yellow jacket' really meant.

As soon as the General had gone to bed, alone with her son, she said:

'Charles, what was it really like?'

Her son thought for a moment, then said: 'Wait here. I'll show you.'

He vanished, only to reappear five minutes later. The figure that came silently, swiftly, into the Gordon sitting-room was that of a Chinese mandarin wearing the yellow jacket in all its glory with the silks of blue-and-gold embroidery, the skull-cap, and the great long sleeves that completely hid the hands.

He stood there in the centre of the room, the lamplight bringing to life the lustre of the robe, its richness and its exotic grace. For a full minute he stood there, as still as a statue, his face assuming the immobility and pride of a race that was civilized before the West had emerged from barbarism.

Then he broke his pose, moved over to his mother, kissed her, and said good night.

Invitations poured in asking 'Chinese Gordon', who had become a celebrity overnight, to a great variety of functions.

There were cards from Devonshire House, from Downing Street and from the Lord Mayor. Gordon declined them all, bringing himself to write those polite letters of refusal that always irritated him. Deliberately he refused to be lionized, set his heart against 'cashing in' on the legend of 'Chinese Gordon' to advance his career.

When he asked his mother one day where his Chinese journals were she had to confess that a cabinet minister had read them and been so impressed that he had sent them to a printer for limited private publication. Gordon was furious, and, unable to meet the culprit, who was out of London, tracked down the printer and tore up the manuscript with his own hands. His temper, usually carefully controlled, was apt to burst out when anyone tried to make a hero of him.

In 1865 Gordon received the post of officer commanding the Royal Engineers at Gravesend and for six years, until 1871, he sank back gratefully into the obscurity of an army officer with a routine job to do. That job was the replanning and strengthening of the Thames defences, and it is not surprising that Gordon brought to his task novel ideas that caused considerable perturbation in the War Office. But at least they created no publicity, and Gordon could enjoy his new life in the manner he chose.

That manner, to say the least, was unusual for a serving British officer of the day. Fort House became his home, but it also became school, hospital, and refuge for all the needy and desperately poor boys of the district. No one ever turned to Gordon for help and was refused. He really enjoyed helping the unfortunate. Many of the lads he aided by finding them berths on the adventurous cargo ships of Britain that were now beginning to sail in regular schedules to the Americas, to Australia, and to the Far East route of Aden, Singapore, and Shanghai. Gordon kept a large map in his study. It was alive with dozens of little flags pinned to the canvas. Each showed where a Gordon boy was now sailing or working.

After finishing his duties for the day he would come home and change, and after a hot bath and a spartan meal provided by his housekeeper he would conduct evening classes for the boys, who were at that time in transit in his house. They came to him bedraggled, dirty, downcast. They left him clean, decently dressed, and with courage renewed.

When his friends chided him for spending his entire pay on 'these ragamuffins' Gordon retorted that the very fine silver tea-set given to him by Sir William Gordon would realize enough to pay for his funeral. That was all that any man should leave.

This was character, charity, piety, in a manner that nineteenth-century England did not often witness, and never expected from a professional soldier. It did not go quite unremarked. The great and powerful had 'dropped' Gordon after a few months. What was the good of trying to help a man so unworldly, who would neither pay court to the dowagers, nor dance with their daughters?

But the people of Gravesend could not help but appreciate this extraordinary man. Some of them sought him out, and late at night, especially on winter evenings, fanning the coal fire with his favourite bellows that bore his initials and still exists, he would tell his visitor something of his philosophy and thinking. 'None of us deserves praise or honour. We are all sinful, and only by helping others can we purge ourselves of our taint.' It was a gloomy, almost masochistic creed, but Gordon held it fervently.

Stories of his benevolence escaped the curtain of secrecy with which he surrounded his good deeds. He had a gold medal given him by the Empress of China which he cherished for its inscription. One day it disappeared. What had become of it? Gordon had had the inscription erased and had sent it to Canon Miller for the relief of those suffering from the cotton famine in Manchester.

It is true that in the sixties and seventies poverty in England was inconceivable by present-day standards. But the fact remains that the public at large, especially the wealthy, and even the Church, regarded it as a static, 'natural' phenomenon. 'The poor are always with us.' It was the unique reaction of Gordon to fight against these conditions and to help in a practical way as many young people as he could. 'It is not their fault,' he would say, 'that society is as it is. We must help them to help themselves.'

He had a large and well-stocked garden, and at first his friends thought that at least this was his own. But it was not. It was parcelled out, piece by piece, to the very poor so that they could grow fresh vegetables and fruit for their children.

In September 1871 Gordon was appointed British representative on the European Commission on the Danube with headquarters at Galatz. The *Gravesend Herald* risked Gordon's displeasure by writing a leader of appreciation of Gordon, not as a soldier, but as a citizen.

The language and the prose style may seem to us stilted, even pompous, but there is no mistaking the sincerity of a tribute.

'Our readers, without exception, will learn with regret of the departure of Lt.-Col. Gordon from this town where he has resided for six years, gaining a name for the most exquisite charity that will be long remembered. . . .'

The *Herald* was in part appeased for the loss of Gordon by the fact that his successor was an aristocrat, the Honourable G. Wrottersley, but the people of Gravesend knew that they had lost a friend such as they were never likely to have again.

At the 'ragged schools' in particular, Gordon was remembered and is still remembered. For many years on his birthday these schools for poor boys displayed some fine Chinese flags in silk and gold that Gordon had given them, and it was clear that this unusual soldier had become a hero in the hearts of the young people of Gravesend.

From time to time during his sojourn in Gravesend the Press remembered Gordon, especially when there were 'difficulties' in any part of Her Majesty's vast domains. The Queen was now Queen of most of Africa as well as of India. Five hundred million people, it was said, of all colours, castes, and faiths, owed her allegiance. Often 'the natives' appeared to appreciate the benefits of British rule—communications, cleanliness, candour, and an incorruptible judicial system. But sometimes the British Raj was not appreciated. The recipients of our benevolent autocracy were known to declare that they wanted to own their own land and run their own country in their own way, and this in spite of the axiomatic fact that we could run it better than they could. Whenever this happened and the flag was in jeopardy, or young men were being butchered, the papers were apt to say, in that irritating way the Press have: 'Ah, this would never have happened if Gordon had been there. Why is no use made of him? Any engineer can revise the Medway fortifications.'

Perhaps because there was a deal of truth in both assumptions, those in power in the Army were determined not to be moved. England was still in the stranglehold of a small, immensely powerful, and wealthy ruling class,[1] largely related by marriage, and determined not to be dictated to by anyone, least of all by Fleet Street.

So Gordon's 'promotion', when it did come, made no use whatever of his remarkable gifts, though it did use his experiences on the Danube Commission. The appointment was therefore difficult to criticize except on the ground that Gordon's talents would be as wasted in Turkey as they had been in Gravesend. It is difficult to avoid the conclusion that those at the top were intent on deflating the Gordon legend. It may have been the duty of a comparatively junior officer and gentleman to be a hero, but he should be a quiet hero, not one who constantly attracted the limelight from his superiors. Certainly Gordon had tried hard to be the unknown Englishman, but his exploits made this impossible. His name rang a bell in England, so that when men thought of him they thought of courage, daring, and the legend of a leader of men.

The Press had wanted Gordon sent to South Africa to 'pacify' the Ashanti who were proving very troublesome. A wind of change, the first of its kind, was blowing through the great continent. Gordon's appointment to Galatz put an end to any such heroics.

But, as fate would have it, it was Africa that claimed Gordon.

The Turkish Empire, which of course included Egypt, and its ruler the Khedive, had an able and urbane representative on the Danube Commission, a man named Nubar Pasha, an official of the old school. Gordon greatly impressed this man, and Nubar Pasha asked Gordon to recommend an officer of engineers to succeed Sir Samuel Baker as governor of the tribes in Upper Egypt. A year later Gordon offered his own services. The Khedive

---

[1] I do not mean to infer that this oligarchy was wicked, but sometimes it was selfish.

applied to the British Government for Gordon to be seconded to his service.

The authorities in London decided—not too reluctantly—to let Gordon go, and in the summer of 1873 he left Galatz and returned briefly to London. Having completed his personal and official preparations, he sailed for Cairo en route for his new post.

On reaching Cairo he was told that the Khedive himself wished to see him. He was kept waiting for an hour in the gilt-and-silver halls of the Abdin Palace, then summoned into the presence of His Highness. For the first time the Khedive and Gordon met. It was a meeting pregnant with the promise of great events.

IO

His Highness the Khedive

THE title of Khedive was a new one for the ruler of Egypt. Derived from the Persian word *khidiv*, it meant 'sovereign'. It is significant that until the Sultan granted this title to Ismail the Sultan's representative in Cairo—more or less independent of the Porte—had been known as vali or viceroy. It indicated the tendency of the sultans to grant more and more autonomy to Egypt. This attitude had been partly forced upon them by an astounding man, Mohammed Ali, who had been a pasha in 1811 but had led a successful revolt against the Mamaluke Dynasty and confirmed it by murdering nearly all the Beys in Egypt at that time. Apart from this, Mohammed Ali was most reluctant to acknowledge the overlordship of the Sultan, though he did so in form at any rate. He strengthened his position by conquering most of the Sudan and the whole Nile Valley, staking Egypt's ancient claim to be lords of the Nile from its source to its delta.

It was the grandson of this remarkable man, the Khedive Ismail, who, on the advice of Nubar Pasha, had agreed to employ Gordon in the place of Sir Samuel Baker, the former governor of the southern provinces of Egypt.

Ismail Pasha was a man of kingly bearing, exquisite manners, and high intelligence. He was not a man of honour in the Western sense for he had been brought up in the tradition of absolutism which meant that what the Khedive wanted was right and was in fact the law. As the Khedive wanted different things at different times his policies were regarded as tortuous by foreigners, and his promises not worth the paper they were written on. To the Khedive it seemed absurd that he should ever be asked to give undertakings to foreigners, and if he was so importuned his good manners got the better of him and he graciously concurred without any intention of carrying out his promise.

Nevertheless Ismail was probably the best khedive Egypt had had for a very long time. He was enlightened and modern-minded in certain ways. He might torture an insolent servant, but this smooth, sleek, intelligent man in his early forties had transformed the stinking, ill-lit, fever-ridden capital of Cairo.

It was under Ismail and largely as a result of his foresight that the Suez Canal was opened,[1] a feat that greatly increased the world stature and strategic importance of Egypt. Twelve hundred miles of railway were also opened and postal and telegraphic communications set up over the whole country. Nearly half a million acres of land were reclaimed by modern irrigation projects. Sugar and cotton became major crops and modern sugar-refining factories were established. Ports, harbours, and light-houses were built and the Port of Alexandria modernized at a cost of over a million pounds. Cairo itself now became a city of good streets—amply lit—theatres, bandstands, public gardens, and good hotels.

For all or most of this the active brain of Ismail had been responsible. A few years after this, disaster overtook him because he plunged more and more heavily into debt and his creditors were the European powers, in particular France and Britain. International philanthropy, the duty of the rich nations to aid the poorer ones, had not yet been conceived as an idea or a principle. The Khedive's creditors were ruthless, and eventually they brought about his fall.

But in the spring of 1873 everything was still fair in the Egyptian garden. The prestige of Ismail was great. The coffers of Egypt had been kept replenished at first by ivory from the Sudan and then by 'black ivory', the slave trade which was found to be far more profitable than ivory or sugar or even cotton. True

[1] Ismail supported Lesseps throughout all the hazards and difficulties of his great enterprise.

the European slavers had had to withdraw under the pressure of an international outcry against slavery and the vile cruelties practised in the capture of the slaves, their transportation, and their subsequent employment, but this had merely meant that the Arab slavers had taken over. They were more ruthless than the Europeans had been, taking the captives at an earlier age, fourteen or under, and treating them abominably to break their spirits and accustom them to the life of subjugation which they were to lead.

The fate of the thousands of slaves who made this traffic did not worry Ismail at all. Slavery had been a tradition in Egypt since before Moses, his treasury reaped fat rewards from the slavers who were now officially licensed by the Government and paid their dues in return for a specific territory in which they were granted rights of exploitation. But recently the Khedive's attitude towards slavery had undergone a drastic change. This change was due mainly to the rising power of a man named Zobeir, known appropriately enough as the Black Pasha. The Black Pasha was now the acknowledged master of thirty trading and slaving stations, he lived in a palace of his own design in kingly opulence with a large number of wives and concubines, and when the Khedive sent one of his officers, General Bellal, to 'cut him down to size' he routed Bellal and was more powerful than ever. The Khedive had been forced to accept him as an ally in his invasion of Dafour and had, most reluctantly, made him a pasha. But this did not satisfy Zobeir, who now decided that he wanted to be Governor-General of the Sudan. This the Khedive could not allow. A man of the type of Zobeir would be Governor-General in name only. In fact he would be King.

So that the Khedive now had very definite ideas of the role Gordon should play in Equatorial Sudan. He should restore the authority of the Khedive, put the slavers in their place, and re-open the gratifying flow of payments into the exchequer from the Sudan. The Khedive did not want to suppress slavery. . . . He thought that that was absurd, impossible, and against the natural order of things, but he was prepared to *pretend* that the abolition of slavery was his objective until the slavers had all accepted his overlordship, for such an attitude would impress the foreigners—

who were becoming more powerful every day—and might even be necessary to enlist the co-operation of high-minded Englishmen such as Colonel Gordon, who were always talking about freedom and the rights of man to equality and happiness.

Nubar Pasha, of course, was determined to impress Gordon with his own importance and thought, in the tradition of the East, that Gordon should be grateful to him for introducing Gordon to the Khedive. Gordon, unfortunately, was not that kind of man. He was capable of real gratitude towards those who aided him or befriended him, but he saw no reason why he should be indebted to Nubar Pasha as presumably Nubar's master the Khedive needed him, or he would not have sent for him.

Later Gordon was to develop patience and a very real understanding of the importance of Eastern manners when dealing with pashas and slavers alike. He wrote to his mother: 'It is just no use losing patience here or getting angry. One can achieve nothing by it.' Nevertheless he was a quick-tempered man and was apt to explode until the end. At this time, let us face it, he was more than a little self-righteous and unbending. Nubar Pasha irritated him almost unendurably by getting him to wait for a day in an ante-room next to the Khedive's reception-apartments. In the end, after a hot and exasperating delay of many hours, Nubar blandly said: 'His Highness will see you tomorrow at ten. He is tired now and has gone to the harem.'

Gordon nearly returned to England by the next boat, but he reflected that this would mean the failure of a mission before it had begun, and was really unworthy of him. He contained himself and presented himself the next day with that fanatical punctuality that he retained throughout his life. At a minute to ten he was waiting again in his full-dress uniform for the audience. The Khedive did not see him until eleven o'clock, but then he was admitted, the obsequious Nurba Pasha ushering the erect, magnetic little figure into the presence of His Highness.

From this moment Gordon's difficulties were over. He and Ismail were opposites. Gordon was uncompromising, blunt, but with an unpredictable streak of enthusiasm and vision. The Khedive was sophisticated, urbane, witty, and a man of immense charm. They liked each other at once.

Gordon had little time for underlings, and this no doubt accounted for his anger with Nubar Pasha, but the Khedive was no underling. True the Sultan was his overlord, but their relationship was governed by firmans of the Porte and in fact the Khedive was Lord of Egypt in all internal matters.

'Your Highness, this is Colonel Gordon, Royal Engineers, to whom you have graciously granted an audience.'

Gordon bowed, and the Khedive started to discuss business.

'First, Colonel Gordon, your salary . . .'

This surprised Gordon. First, surely, should come the nature and extent of his duties. Salary was a secondary consideration. But he listened while the Khedive, in that soft, insinuating voice of his, suggested that £10,000 a year would be a suitable emolument for his new governor.

Gordon said at once that he had been paid £2,000 a year for his work on the Danube Commission, that this was the salary to which his rank entitled him while on seconded service from the British Army, and that this was the salary he would accept.

The Khedive showed no outward sign of the surprise which he felt. No one ever before had offered him service for a fifth of the pay offered. Nubar Pasha registered frank incredulity. But the Khedive said:

'As you wish, Colonel Gordon, but the position of governor always entails expense and if you find you need more you must apply to me. . . .'

This Gordon agreed to do. The Khedive went on to speak of the slavers, of Zobeir in particular. They could be brought to heel, of course, but it would require a man of resolution to do it. That was why he had sent for Gordon, whose reputation as a resolute and audacious commander was well known. If Ismail was indulging in flattery he was a very skilled dealer in that commodity and Gordon decided he liked and, up to a point, trusted the Khedive.

Gordon, allowed now to speak, expressed the view that nothing would redound more to the good name of Egypt than the wiping out of the abominable trade in slaves, and to this the Khedive nodded his smiling concurrence. Gordon took this to be a mandate to deal with the slavers in his own way, but he was too shrewd not to have his doubts about the real intentions of the Khedive.

'I think the mission is probably a sham,' he wrote home to impress the outside world, 'but we shall see. . . .'

The two men were together for a little over an hour. Then the Khedive withdrew, wishing Gordon good fortune and promising him all support. 'We are friends, Colonel Gordon,' he concluded. The astute Khedive had won the loyalty of a most valuable servant. It was a good morning's work.

Gordon persuaded himself that the Khedive had given him a mandate to stamp out slavery wherever he found it in the million square miles of the Sudan. The Khedive had seen at once that, to secure Gordon's allegiance, he would have to give him some kind of crusade to carry to success. The obliteration of slavery— what a wonderful crusade that would appear to be to Gordon. Clearly he was a man who cared nothing for money. He was one of those rare characters who was only happy when attempting to accomplish the impossible, preferably in uncomfortable circumstances. The Khedive had played his cards very cleverly. He thought that Gordon would be the scourge he needed to bring the slavers into line, and he was right. The difficulty was to call off Gordon once he had embarked on a venture of this kind. In any case Ismail, who in recent months had become really frightened by the growing wealth and arrogance of the chief slave-dealers, was happy that he had this very odd Englishman who, in a day or so, would be setting out for Upper Egypt.

Gordon wished to proceed on his way without fuss, but Nubar Pasha, a nuisance to the end, insisted that as governor-designate of Upper Egypt he must go in state. A large number of servants were engaged, but Gordon instructed these to follow him, and with an equerry departed for Suez where a special train awaited him. To his delight this train broke down and he had to travel by the public train. He reached Suakin on the 25th of February.

From Suakin Gordon was to travel for two weeks to Berber with the two hundred troops assigned to him. He welcomed this, for with recollections of the 'Ever Victorious Army' he rightly thought that the men would get to know him very much better in the desert. It was the first of Gordon's camel-rides and he had

G

not yet acquired the mastery of this difficult form of transport. 'The first two days,' he said, 'were hell. After that it was much better.'

Gordon had insisted on taking into his service a prisoner of the Khedive, Abou Saoud, an ex-slaver with an unsavoury reputation for chicanery. Gordon thought that this man, with his intimate knowledge of the Sudan and the tracks which the slavers' caravans were accustomed to follow, might be of the greatest use to him. Gordon had a high regard for information, and in order to get it was prepared to employ spies. There was, he pointed out, no other way in which a governor could learn what was going on. Nubar Pasha, of course, protested loudly against Gordon taking Abou Saoud with him, but in this instance Gordon had his way.

It was a sign of the respect or the fear which Abou Saoud inspired in Upper Egypt that he was known there as 'the Sultan'.

Gordon's party left Berber on the 9th of March and arrived in Khartoum by boat on the 12th. He had now collected a band of workers who formed his staff. These were Romulus Gessi, an able Italian and a man of courage whom Gordon had known in the Crimea, Mr Kemp, an engineer, and a Mr Russell, Mr Anson, Mr Long, an American, and the terrifying figure of Abou Saoud, who looked more and more bloodthirsty as he approached his old hunting-grounds.

The plan was that each was to shoulder the responsibility for some portion of Gordon's vast area. For instance, Colonel Long was to take charge of Gondokoro, Gessi and Anson were sent to the Bahr Gazelle, while 'the Sultan' was to stay with his master and to be his eyes and ears.

Khartoum greeted Gordon with full honours. The Governor-General met him, a band played, and salutes were taken. But Gordon was determined to stay no more than ten days in the capital. Especially as he was given good news. The 'sudd', a malignant, grassy growth in the river, had been cleared by the soldiers so that the journey from Khartoum to Gondokoro, which had taken Sir Samuel Baker the best part of a year, could now be accomplished in a matter of weeks.

Nor did Gordon waste his time in Khartoum. While waiting to leave and with the consent of the Governor-General—who had heard that the Khedive liked Gordon—Gordon issued the follow-ing decree. As it is a foreword of so much that was to follow and indicates the scope of the mission with which Gordon thought he had been charged it is worth quoting in full.

'HIS HIGHNESS THE KHEDIVE having invested me with authority as Governor of the Provinces of the Equatorial Lakes and in view of past abuses it is DECREED:

'1. That IVORY is a Government monopoly.

'2. That no one may enter the Provinces of the Equatorial Lakes without a "teskere" from the Governor-General of the Sudan and a visa from the Governor of that province.

'3. Armed bands are absolutely forbidden.

'4. The importation of firearms and gunpowder is forbidden.

'5. Whosoever shall disobey this decree shall be punished with the full rigour of military law.'

This curt, clear manifesto was signed simply 'GORDON'.

So in the the first weeks of his mission, before he had even arrived in the great provinces he was to control, Gordon challenged the slavers, the law-breakers, the murderers, and anyone who might be thinking of challenging the authority of the Khedive— or of Gordon.

But the Arab slavers—rich and now powerful—smiled, for these were words only and they had, as yet, no notion what kind of a man it was who had come to rule them.

There were many surprises in store for everyone.

11

'Gordon is Here'

BEFORE Gordon left Khartoum for Gondokoro there was a delightful incident that shows us one side of Gordon's complex character and also throws light on the attitude towards life of the great Egyptian officials in the provinces.

After Gordon had rested—in so far as Gordon was capable of rest or relaxation—the Governor-General decided that he would give the traditional banquet in Gordon's honour. Gordon accepted the invitation. He disliked banquets—'too much food and too much talk'—but it would have been churlish to refuse. Besides, in Gondokoro he would have to rely on the Governor-General to get urgent messages through to the Khedive or to Sir Evelyn Baring, our man in Cairo. So Gordon put on his full mess uniform and turned up at the Palace prepared to put up with the banalities, and even to endure complimentary speeches.

All went well at first. The banquet—men only—was enlivened by some excellent French wine, and the Governor-General spoke of Gordon in terms of kindness and appreciation, without the fulsome flattery Gordon dreaded. Gordon replied briefly and with some humour.

After the banquet, however, came the Governor-General's *pièce de résistance*, the ballet. This was conducted by a troupe of athletic young soldiers—and a team of dancing-girls. Gordon could hardly believe his eyes. The girls were naked. They had none of those little gestures towards restraint that dancers the world over usually adopt. The soldiers and the girls started their dance facing away from each other, but, as the tempo of the music increased, they half turned towards one another and then they intermingled, joining hands. The girls by now were making gestures which could be interpreted only as attempts to seduce the male ballet and the men were making a curious clucking sound of appreciation, indicating that they were not made of stone. The dance was becoming more and more intimate, the leading male dancer and the first dancing-girl were now surrounded by a circle of clapping men and girls, who were clucking and singing to the music. What exactly was going on in the middle of that circle? The beat of the band became more and more insistent. At that moment the Austrian Consul, who had drunk more than a bottle of champagne himself, could bear the suspense no longer. He jumped up and with a whoop of joy crashed into the middle of the circle and was immediately lost to sight as the circle re-formed.

The Governor-General was now singing with the rest of the guests, and half rose in his seat, with the evident intention of following the Austrian Consul on his voyage of exploration. This was too much for Gordon. He got up abruptly and, without a word to his host, left.

The effect of this strange incident was depressing as far as the Governor-General and what might be described as the *corps diplomatique* of Khartoum were concerned. Had they really done anything wrong? The weird little Englishman seemed to think so. But what was the use of drinking a lot of fine and very expensive wine, and working oneself into a happy amorous trance, unless there was some reward for one's whetted appetite? The English were very odd. It was probably their climate, the cold and the fog. It got into their bones so that they could never enjoy themselves. . . .

On the other hand Gordon's gesture probably stood him in good stead. It made it quite clear to one and all that he was not as other men were. If Africa could not corrupt him the Governor-General might, secretly, have an added respect for him. The whole of Khartoum knew the next day that the new Englishman had quit the Palace party. The rumour ran through the dust-laden street along the Nile bank to the barracks. It flashed down the dirty lanes that led to the market. The legend of Gordon had sown its first seeds in Khartoum.

Nevertheless, Gordon was delighted on the 22nd of March to set sail for Gondokoro. He had nothing in common with the pleasure-loving, womanizing little circle of top Khartoum officials. He was glad to be on his way to his own empire.

The days on the Nile, en route for Gondokoro, gave Gordon time to reflect on all that had happened to him in the last few weeks since he had set foot in Africa. Had he made many mistakes? Was it a mistake to leave the Governor-General's party, as he had done, to express his displeasure at the ballet? He thought not. Some standards had to be maintained. How was one to control and rule these people unless they thought that one had a higher moral code? Was it not, in fact, the whole difference between the Christian and the Moslem? The Mohammedan faith stressed pleasure hereafter for those who kept the law, and most of the faithful tried to anticipate some of that pleasure in this world rather than wait for the next. The Christian was a different kind of person. Christianity stressed piety, chastity, the dignity of self-denial. No, surely he had been right.

Certainly he had made a friend of the Khedive. That was his chief gain since coming to Egypt. Ismail—courted, still rich— was now all-powerful. True, his motives for appearing to suppress slavery were suspect. Probably he realized that he could borrow more and more money from European governments only if he appeared to join their queer campaign for the abolition of slavery. . . . And the richness and almost sensuous atmosphere of the Abdin Palace—which Ismail had built for himself to his own design—had offended Gordon.

He had been shown by Nubar Pasha, intent on impressing him, the Khedive's diamond-studded dinner-service in virgin gold. Gordon had secretly thought it vulgar, and so it was, but its barbaric magnificence fitted in very well with the opulence and sophistication of the new Egypt. He was shown the Opera House —new, of course—for which Verdi had written *Aida*. And he was shown the Khedive's collection of *objets d'art* that included some deliciously expensive and quite useless pieces, the work of the

Russian Court jewellers—a rose-coloured egg set in lapis lazuli that contained a horoscope of the Grand Duchess for whom it had been designed, and a pair of candlesticks joined together by a lovers' knot in pure gold.[1] These extravagances Gordon now remembered as the long days on the river merged one into the next.

What perturbed him most were the rumours he had heard that the Khedive's men were constantly, on one pretext or another, seizing lands to add to the private fortune of their master, while the land taxes, extorted by the lash, were every year increased to offset Ismail's rapidly growing debts. The Khedive was now said to own nearly a quarter of Egypt personally. Then of course there were those endless inner apartments of the Palace that Nubar Pasha had merely hinted at, the harem rooms where the Egyptian, French, Armenian, and Italian ladies of the harem, scented and cosseted, awaited their lord's pleasure. It was all very unhealthy, really.

Fortunately, Gordon had liked the Khedive personally, so much so that, as he sailed for Gondokoro, he felt that, whatever happened, he had a real friend at the summit.

This was Gordon's first close contact with the Nile. He watched the river from dawn, when the sun seemed to spring out of a cloudless sky, to the evening when it sank with red regality. The Nile was wide and—at first—smooth, strong, and silent. But that silence was relieved by the life that abounded on its banks. The banks were densely wooded, these first few days, with tamarind and gum trees. Storks, pelicans, and egrets strutted on the banks, calling it seemed to the passing ship, derisively, perhaps, at anyone who imagined that they could do any good by going to Gondokoro. Big game, too, was much more common than it is now, and the crocodiles on the mud-banks looked like drift-logs of wood, unless one went close enough to see their wicked, bloodshot eyes glinting in the sun.

For the first time Gordon felt a communion with the great river. Here was reality in the midst of human artificiality. Here was strength and purpose and primeval wisdom. Gordon felt he drew strength from the river, and his active, taut mind, for ever

[1] King Farouk inherited, and added to, this collection.

conjuring up new situations, was pacified by the rhythm of the
water and the quiet routine of the days.

Typically, meeting a faster steamer at a point six days up
river from Khartoum, Gordon changed to it. He was anxious to
reach his capital 'as quickly and as secretly as possible'. He had
insisted that no messengers to Gondokoro should be sent to
announce his arrival. Sir Samuel Baker had been defeated in the
end by the dysentery, the malaria, the excessive heat, and the
atmosphere of utter hopelessness that seemed to live in the very
sand and stones of the station. And when he left he had handed
over to an Egyptian subordinate. At least Baker had organized
some kind of central living-quarters. He had laid out some
gardens, run up the crescent green flag of the Khedive, and paid
the troops with regularity. Gordon suspected that all this had
now been abandoned. But if the Egyptian garrison knew he was
coming there would be an attempt to veneer over the rottenness
of any abuses that had crept in. Hence Gordon's plan to appear
from out of the blue, round a bend of the river, with the Khedive's
mandate in his pocket. He thought that in arriving unannounced
he might discover the real state of affairs. Nor was he to be disappointed.

Gordon's reception along the banks of the river, at the
hamlets opposite which his steamer anchored for the night,
varied significantly according to the interests of the inhabitants.
At the entrance to the Saubat River, where the steamer halted to
cut more wood for fuel, they surprised a tribe of Dinkas who had
encamped by the river to water and feed their camels. All the
men, Gordon noted, were naked, and their table manners left
much to be desired. The chief, not satisfied with his own portion
of food, seized the plate of his aide and ate that portion too.
But the Dinkas were friendly. Before they left they sang a song
to Gordon which no one understood, but which was obviously
complimentary. Then the chief ordered his men to crawl to
Gordon and kiss his feet, a little ceremony that Gordon thought
degrading. . . .

At Bohr, which was in the firm grip of the slavers, the Arabs
were anything but friendly, but to be on the safe side they sent
out a delegation to sing to Gordon after dinner—and perhaps

to spy on him. Gordon spoke to one or two of the Arabs[1] and was impressed by their manliness and fine manners. Though he felt that he and what he stood for was resented, he had to acknowledge that these were men—upright, fearless, believing that Allah would protect them. They were centuries apart from the spirit-worshipping Dinkas.

On the 16th of April, twenty-four days after leaving Khartoum, Gordon's little steamer swept round the river-bend that lies to the north of the station and dropped anchor, to the intense surprise, not to say consternation, of the officials and officers who were running Gondokoro in their own way. They came out, as soon as they could get into their uniforms, to greet Gordon, but it was too late to conceal anything. Gordon, in a matter of days if not of hours, knew just how great was the task he had to tackle, and how far there had been a reversion to the bad old ways of corruption, cruelty, and squalor since Baker had left.

It was worse than even Gordon had anticipated. The neat station which Baker had left had gone to seed. The desert had encroached again. Naouf Bey, the commander of the troops at Gondokoro, was secretly hostile to Gordon and soon became openly resentful and jealous of Abou Saoud who, as soon as he was in sight of the promised land and his old haunts, indulged in a spree of extortion from all and sundry, in the name of his master Gordon.

Baker had paid the troops in cash and with commendable promptness. That, too, was a thing of the past. Now they were being paid, if at all, in spirits and slave-girls. It was like the old days of the 'Ever Victorious Army' all over again. Gordon inspected the whole station and allowed nothing to be hidden from him. So bad was the situation that he, himself, was in danger a mile or so outside the garrison wall. The morning reveille had, of course, been allowed to lapse. The officers were all in bed sleeping off the effects of the evening's debauch or being amused by their slave-girls. Gordon started to busy himself with drastic reform. He was forty-one now, and in high spirits. The more hopeless the situation was, the more of a challenge it presented.

[1] Gordon still had to rely on interpreters; later he was to speak good Arabic, but with an English intonation.

He dismissed all the officials who were dealing with the slavers either as partners or agents. He even dismissed Abou Saoud who had reverted completely to brigandage. In a stern letter of rebuke Gordon reminded the former slaver that he had trusted him and employed him when he was a prisoner in Cairo, but 'now you have become arrogant and corrupt, constantly deceive me, force your way into my private quarters and treat those under my command with contempt, showing yourself an ambitious, grasping man unworthy of my trust'.

Abou Saoud was surprised at his master's firmness, but the real reason for Gordon's action against him was that Gordon rightly suspected that Abou had been guilty of stirring up the troops to revolt. Gordon had a quick eye for the first muttered signs of insubordination and mutiny.[1] No doubt his quick action established him as master in Gondokoro.

Chaille-Long was sent by Gordon to make contact with the Mutesa, the powerful king in Buganda, and Gordon himself steamed back to Khartoum to collect a large quantity of Austrian dollars with which, in future, he was to pay his garrison. Then he made an astounding request to Ismail Pasha Yacoub, the Governor-General, who had been his host at the famous ballet party. Gordon said he wished Equatoria to be treated as an independent state, separated from the Sudan. He pointed out that the people were not Sudanese nor Moslem, and that they should be governed as a separate entity. The Governor-General naturally refused. Gordon then telegraphed to the Khedive in Cairo asking that this should be done. The Khedive considered the matter. It was a startling request. It cut a huge area out of the domain of Khartoum, but, of course, it did not take anything from the Khedive. If this extraordinary man had his way he might be able to restore order in Equatoria and greatly increase the Khedive's revenue, a thought that was always uppermost in the Khedive's mind.

The Khedive's answer was to agree that Gordon should run Equatoria 'as part of my domains, as you see fit'. It was a major victory. Gordon was now undisputed ruler of an area as great as

---

[1] Gordon developed a perception of treachery that was uncanny, and stood him in good stead.

France. Yet ahead of him lay appalling hazards. To the south the country was unmapped and unexplored. The climate was almost unbearable, and the tribes, in all directions, had been antagonized by the abominable behaviour of the garrison.

Gordon was faced with a task greater than any he had had to tackle in China. The days of supreme test lay ahead.

12

Everything is Possible

GORDON'S three years of service as Governor of Upper Egypt from 1874 to 1877 were probably the best years of his life. He had not, of course, the great power he was to wield later as Governor-General of the Sudan, but the Equatorial Lakes was a vast district, largely unexplored, providing every kind of obstacle, an atrocious climate, hostile tribes and slavers, and every kind of natural hazard, including the cataracts that made the river an angry barrier above Gondokoro, apart from the giant hippopotami that imperilled the boats in the calmer stretches.

Gordon brought not only comparative peace to this great area; he procured, as we have seen, its recognition as an independent territory. His work lived on and the Government of the Sudan today is now faced with the problem of how best to unite a largely Christian and pagan south with the main Moslem body of the country. Gordon's answer to that problem—which, of course, fitted in with the extension of his own power—was to treat Upper Egypt as an autonomous part of the Khedive's kingdom. Gordon may have been right, but the final answer of history has not yet been given.

In addition to this major administrative change, that enabled Gordon to by-pass the Governor-General, Ismail Pasha Yacoub, in Khartoum and deal with Cairo direct, Gordon began operations to the south that had as their objective no less a goal than shifting the whole Egyptian administration to a more central point in

Africa and, by establishing a force at Mombasa Bay and planting the flag of the Khedive on the Great Lakes, to encircle Abyssinia, with which country Egypt was at war. These were tremendous projects. Fortunately for Gordon they had the grandiose, triumphant ring that appealed to Ismail in Cairo. This was Empire with a grand design. Though the Khedive could send the most irritating and vacillating telegrams (which were apt to provoke an offer to resign from Gordon), on the whole the Khedive supported Gordon. The fact that he did so greatly increased Gordon's waxing prestige.

In all Near Eastern and African countries the chief officials are apt to be divided into those whose power and influence is declining and those whose prestige is mounting. During these three years Gordon was certainly in the latter category. It was high noon for Colonel Gordon.

Before Gordon could tackle the ambitious major designs he had in mind for his master, the Khedive, he had a lot of hard work to do on an administrative and provincial level, and this work included a number of spectacular raids on the camps of slavers, but before he could even venture on these raids of retribution he had to secure his own safety and that of his staff and the soldiers under his overall command.

One of his first moves was to move the administration from Gondokoro, which was infested with marsh fever, to Lardo nearby, which was considerably higher and very much healthier. He then set to work to restore order out of chaos.

During this time Gordon would awake at dawn, drink some coffee, open his Bible, and read in peace for ten minutes. Then he would bathe, dress, and stride out to tackle the day. He was the incarnation of energy. He was the complete opposite to the attitude of *Insha Allah*, if God is willing. When Gordon said something had to be done it had to be done. No excuses were accepted.

The Arabs were amazed by this fantastic little man. They watched him as he would leave his divan, from which he gave judgment in any disputes, and head, with a most un-African haste, towards the most difficult task he had on hand at that moment. They had a name for him, 'The Little Khedive', and it reflected their opinion that in the hands of this man was absolute authority.

A member of his staff writing home after Gordon had been in Equatoria just over half a year wrote:

'Gordon has done wonders since his stay in this country. When he arrived he found seven hundred soldiers in Gondokoro who dare not venture beyond the walls except in large parties because of the enmity of the tribes whom Baker had antagonized. Now he has garrisoned seven stations—at Saubat, Bohr, Lardo, Rageef, Fatiko, Duffli, and Makrake. Baker's "expedition" cost the Government £1,170,347. Gordon has already remitted to Khartoum enough cash to cover his expenses.'

He made friends with the troops by entertaining them. This was not too difficult. Gordon was an engineer and he used his training to devise amusement. He had a magnetic exploder that would fire a gun a hundred yards away. He had a magnesium-wire light, and he had brought with him a magic lantern that showed views of London and even pictures of the Great Queen, as well as some more recent pictures taken in Cairo including a very useful one of His Highness the Khedive shaking hands with Colonel Gordon!

There were few visitors from Khartoum to the south in those days but anyone who did make the journey towards the end of the first year of Gordon's governorship would have remarked on the startling change in the country. Gordon, by this time, had made friends with a large number of powerful tribal chiefs; he had put the fear of God into the slavers by the most formidable raids on their cattle, the only retaliation that really hurt them; and along the river stretched those neat, British-type military stations with their carefully cultivated fields of maize, their whitewashed walls, their bugle-calls at morning and as the sun went down, and their ceremony of hoisting the Egyptian flag at dawn and lowering it before nightfall. These creations of Gordon—the military outposts—worked like clockwork, and Gordon could now be reasonably certain that if he swooped down on one of them, without being announced, as was his habit, he would find his officer in charge pressing on with the ideas Gordon had given him. Gordon's men began to take a pride in their appearance. They were becoming

less and less like the 'Ever Victorious Army' every day and more
like Her Majesty's Royal Engineers. . . .

Baker had pursued a policy of shooting all those who stood
in his way, slavers and 'unfriendly' tribesmen alike. It was a
disastrous policy. Gordon at once reversed it. First, invariably,
he tried to make friends. If he was able to do this he introduced
money as a means of exchange and even set up a store in each of
his stations. But if he was repulsed, and the delinquent was
known to be either plotting a revolt or dealing in slaves, Gordon
organized one of his lightning raids on the culprit's cattle and
women. This had great advantages. No one was killed. The
offender lost his sole means of livelihood; and that could be
restored to him if he repented. Gordon was a great believer in
political conversion. In China he had seen how former rebels
were glad to join his ranks and swell the forces of the 'Ever
Victorious Army'. He used the same methods now. In the one
hand was the lash, in the other the carrot. You could either live
as an enemy of Gordon, and lose your cattle and perhaps your
wives and daughters, or you could live as a friend of Gordon
and go in peace.[1] It surprised Gordon himself how many of his
enemies chose to come over to him. Always the cattle and the
women—they were valued in that order—were returned to the
convert, and if Gordon thought the conversion genuine he
would even return the calves born in captivity, claiming no
usufruct.

But this weapon that Gordon developed to pacify the equatorial
empire of the Khedive can be fully appreciated only if we watch
a raid, its reason, and its culmination, in progress and at very
close quarters.

One of the first powerful chiefs suspected both of slaving and
of being an ally of the Black Pasha was a man named Bedden.
His territory lay close to Gordon's headquarters and his activities
were an affront to Gordon's authority which, of course, represented
the authority of the Khedive. Gordon sent a messenger to Bedden
requesting him to report to Gordon so that they might arrive at
an understanding. The messenger returned with a brief note

[1] Gordon's methods now seem to us drastic. At the time they were considered
humane. Incidentally he appears to have had no colour prejudice.

which, being translated, read: 'If you send another messenger he will be put to death.'

It was war.

Gordon trained his men much as commandos are now trained. They travelled very light, moved noiselessly and at night, even smeared their faces with a black-green substance to camouflage their features. Some of the Sudanese needed no such protection, but there were a number of fair men among the Egyptians, the officers in particular.

The cattle at night were herded into *seribas*, the local version of the African kraal. On this occasion, at four in the morning, leaving the main party within call, a small contingent fired a fusillade of shots at the entrance to the *seriba*. As was anticipated the guards fled in panic, hardly having time to beat their war-drums.

The cattle, a huge herd of over two thousand head, were captured without a fight and Gordon's men on horseback, riding on their flanks, herded them back to the compound Gordon had built for such purposes. In this action Gordon had received valuable information from a friendly sheik and he did not hesitate to reward the sheik with some of Bedden's cattle. As dawn was breaking the war-drums did sound, but half-heartedly, and no major action developed as a result of Gordon's lightning raid.

Gordon was delighted with the success of this operation, which was the prelude to many others, so that before long the chief slavers took care to have their permanent quarters outside Gordon's provinces and only to enter by stealth, to seize their victims, and then to move out as rapidly and as secretly as they had come. Even then they knew that Gordon had the power and prestige to adopt tactics of 'hot pursuit' to the north or to the south and, in order to prevent expensive disaster, the slavers had to maintain a constant watch on Gordon's movements and activities, so that his camp was always surrounded by unseen spies who reported his slightest move.

These cattle-raids now have an unexpected, almost ferocious ring about them, but Gordon was convinced that they were the only means whereby he could achieve his end, namely, that he

The Mahdi's primitive arsenal

The Maxim gun that eventually subdued the Dervishes of the Mahdi

Gordon's telescope, made by Callaghan & Co. of New Bond Street; Gordon bought it second-hand for £5 in Khartoum market and used it to scan the Nile bend for the relief that never came in the siege of Khartoum. (Discovered by Gerald Sparrow in a cellar of the Palace)

should be regarded with such fear and respect that no hand would be raised against the laws which he, himself, in the name of the Khedive, had promulgated. 'One must be feared,' he wrote, 'or one can achieve nothing.'

Gordon's grandest design of all, the shifting of the administrative centre of the Khedive's rule to a more central point in Africa, met with great opposition in the British Press when it leaked out that such a project was in the wind. Mr Gladstone was bitterly opposed to it. The Cabinet as a whole disliked it and the Khedive, who now was sinking month by month into deeper debt, had to submit to the pressure of his creditor governments to withdraw the ships he had sent to Mombasa Bay, and in the end to call off the whole project.

With his ambition to probe the true sources of the Nile, which the Geographical Society had pressed Gordon to undertake, for it was the greatest geographical mystery of the day, Gordon achieved far more. He did not solve the problem with any certainty, but he got much nearer a solution than had ever been reached before, and his officers, Gessi in particular, made maps that were reliable and accurate of great stretches of the river that, up to then, had been indicated on the maps more with optimistic divination than any conviction of fact.

Gordon's men tackled the river first in *nuggars*, immensely strong locally built boats made to withstand both the torrents and rocks of the cataracts and the charges of the hippopotami, who were quite fearless and charged immediately if disturbed. But these small boats were no real solution to opening up Nile navigation. In the end, by taking his steamers to pieces below the cataracts and assembling them above, Gordon achieved the seemingly impossible and had both the *Nyanza* and the *Khedive* on Lake Victoria. He had mapped the Nile to within a day's march of its source, though this he did not know.

The Nile kept her secret from the probing of Gessi and his friend Carlo Piaggia. These two men discovered that the Nile did indeed lead to Lake Albert, and Gessi had circumnavigated the lake to discover that it was very much smaller than Sir Samuel Baker had reported. Moreover the stretch of the Nile that led to the lake was broad and smooth, stretching through the country

H

like an emerald necklace—a fascinating spectacle, and peaceful after the roar and thunder of the cataracts.

However, both the Italians claimed that they had discovered rivers of great volume that branched off from the main river; or were they in fact the main stream?

One of these reported rivers was said to be just north of Lake Albert, the other at the mouth of Lake Kyoga. Gordon tried to solve the problem himself in an expedition on water and by forced marches, but his men trespassed into the territory of the great African king Mutesa and were kept as hostages for some months. In the end the river refused to give up the secret of where she was born.

After nearly three years of service in Equatoria Gordon felt his energy ebbing, and from time to time experienced periods of melancholia. He had a ridiculous quarrel with Gessi who was warm-hearted, loyal, sensitive, and brave. Gessi thought that his services had not been sufficiently rewarded in the honours which from time to time both the Egyptian and British governments sent to those on seconded service. Gordon turned to Gessi and said: 'What a pity you are not an Englishman!' It was a stupid remark, unlike Gordon at his best. But it was a very natural one. Gordon belonged to a generation and a class that were sincerely sorry that foreigners who had proved themselves worthy could not enjoy the immense prestige of being British. Gordon had no sooner made his remark than Gessi exploded in a gust of Italian fury, throwing his cap at Gordon and resigning on the spot. But Gordon and Gessi were comrades as well as friends. In a few days they had healed the breach and were able to laugh at the incident.

Gordon surveyed what he had accomplished, and in his heart he must have known that he had done more than perhaps anyone else could have accomplished in the circumstances. Yet he was not satisfied. He could not pretend that he had smashed slavery. That evil snake had merely slid out of his grasp to attack where and when it could. Its hideous trail still stretched across the Sudan. The people still went in fear. The Khedive, as he moved deeper and deeper into debt, had his freedom of choice and decision ever more circumscribed, and Sir Evelyn Baring, whom

Gordon detested—an offensive stuck-up little man tied to his desk was Gordon's conception of him, by no means a fair one—became daily more powerful and intent on keeping Gordon well within his terms of reference, an ambition that no one had yet been able to achieve.

The climate sapped Gordon's body and mind although, by a miracle it seemed, he kept free of fever or indeed any illness. It was more the feeling that vast and unseen powers were working against him that made Gordon have his fits of morbidity.

At these times he would retire into his tent, putting up outside the black flag and hatchet that were the sign that on no account was he to be disturbed. Gordon had good reason for wanting to be alone, for he would remain for as much as a day and a night alone with his Bible fighting his private, personal war, the war of his spirit. He was convinced that he was personally tempted and had a weakness that craved to give in to all kinds of evil, to sadism and cruelty, to unnatural love, to self-indulgence, to arrogance and the love of power.[1]

At this time he seemed indeed possessed. Before he emerged from his session with his Maker Gordon's little body would shake and be convulsed. He would lie there panting until, it seemed, the evil spirit left him, and a great peace descended on him. Then he rested and next morning, again clear-eyed, brisk, energetic, once more the Governor would go about his duties.

Yet Gordon was tired, for never in this first period of service did he allow himself so much as a single day's holiday. He travelled back to Cairo with Gessi. They were friends again now. On reaching London Gordon sent in his resignation to the Khedive, thanking him for his friendship and support, but saying that he was weary.

'I would like to be rid of General Gordon,' he told friends.

But it was not to be. Gordon was to return in triumph as Governor-General of the Sudan and reach the pinnacle of his fame. He was also to enter the phase in which he became a major figure in world affairs. A struggle of momentous consequences to Britain and her Empire was to develop between Gordon and the

---

[1] Strachey's suggestion that these periods of self-castigation were accompanied by drinking-bouts seems to be a cruel libel on Charles Gordon.

Khedive on one hand and Gladstone's Liberal administration, represented by Baring in Cairo, on the other.

Gordon had yet to live with General Gordon for a number of years until, with the certainty and dread of a Greek drama, the last act was to be written in blood.

13

The Governor-General

WHEN it became known in London that Gordon had decided not to return to Africa, the newspapers, *The Times* in particular, urged that his unique gifts should be used nearer home. 'He should', said *The Times*, 'be appointed Governor of Bulgaria. He would soon make that turbulent Province as peaceful as an English county.'

Many of *The Times* readers liked the idea, and a great volume of letters reached Printing House Square supporting the proposal. Quite a number of the letters related new aspects of Gordon's services during his governorship of Equatoria. The correspondence achieved nothing except that it showed, once again, that Gordon had a solid backing of public opinion behind him in Britain, that he had, as always, the loyal support of Britain's greatest newspaper; and it was widely known that the Queen herself followed the fortunes of General Gordon with close and sympathetic interest.

Ismail, the Khedive, in Cairo woke up to the fact that he might lose the services of the only man he could trust absolutely. When Gordon had taken leave of the Khedive in Cairo he had assured that potentate that one day he would return, and Gordon's telegram of resignation came to the Khedive as a disappointment. He was not surprised, for Gordon was unpredictable. He was a man of moods. He was always consulting God, and God apparently was giving him different answers at different times. This did not imply that Gordon was insincere. He believed completely in his own decisions, made after days of deliberation and communion.

Ismail was not too disturbed. He had always known how to manage Gordon, a secret that very few people took the trouble to learn. After all, verbally, Gordon had promised to come back. The Khedive personally dictated a telegram to Gordon that was a masterpiece of cultured Egyptian craftsmanship:

'I refuse to believe that once Gordon has given his word *as a gentleman* anything will ever induce him to go back on his word.' And the artistry was maintained to the end, for this pregnant message was signed: 'Your affectionate ISMAIL.'

Is it sacrilege to suggest that Gordon had in his make-up a trace of snobbery? If so it was snobbery of the highest order, pure and unadulterated. It was the snobbery of the man who dearly loves an emperor. Ismail had touched on the two points against which Gordon had no defence. The assurance given in Cairo had been verbal, but according to Ismail that made it all the more sacred, for it was the word of a gentleman. And to how many in the world would the Khedive have terminated a message with those beguiling friendly words 'Your affectionate Ismail'?

Gordon capitulated, not too reluctantly. Back in London, after the novelty had worn off, he found his glance wandering, ever more often, towards the great map of Egypt and the Sudan which he kept in his study, and when he did this the Nile, great and gleaming, would creep back into his mind's eye. The Nile in the morning: majestic and strong, cool, serene, clear, irresistible. The Nile at night: dark, secret, purposeful. He felt that always in Egypt the great river had sustained him—and now it was calling him back.

Gordon's resolve to change his mind and return did not prevent him from deciding that he would dictate his own terms. The Khedive, he thought, must be in real difficulties to have called him back so urgently. If he needed him so much, would he not give Gordon the greatest office of all, that of Governor-General of the Sudan? Would he not agree to a firman that publicly proclaimed Gordon's mission to be the restoration of peace to the Khedive's domains, the settlement of the long-drawn-out and angry dispute with Abyssinia, and the complete suppression of slavery?

Gordon made up his mind that he would ask for both the power and the mandate to act on the grandest and most effective scale. Typically, he did not leave the negotiation to his superiors to conduct. He did not consult Sir Evelyn Baring, the British representative in Cairo. He returned to Cairo and sought an audience with the Khedive. This time there was no delay. Gordon passed over the heads of a number of dignitaries who were waiting to see His Highness. Within minutes Ismail and Gordon were together again.

Ismail was delighted to see Gordon. Here he was refreshed and resolute again, the brilliant blue eyes as alert, the bearing as erect, as ever.

'My friend,' said the Khedive, 'it is a joy to have you back.'

Thus greeted, Gordon had to remember resolutely what he had in mind to request. Ismail spoke first, and at length, of his problems. First there was this infuriating dispute with Johannes who had made himself Emperor of Abyssinia. The whole frontier with that country was in dispute—and the Egyptian troops had suffered some humiliating reverses at the hands of 'the black monsters' from across the border. Then there was the problem of the slavers. Gordon had quelled slavery in his province but in other parts of the Sudan, in Dafour in particular, slavery was rampant, and the Khedive was being subjected to great pressure from both London and Paris to do something about it. He was inclined to respond to these exhortations, for the simple reason that the slavers were becoming too big. Look at this man Zobeir Pasha, now in Cairo. He wanted the Khedive to make him Prince of Dafour and to sign an alliance with him. Reports had reached the Khedive of the grandeur of Zobeir's palace. It consisted of a series of courtyards each enclosing the other, and in the centre, in a palace of real magnificence, Zobeir ruled as a king, giving audience daily to hundreds of callers and supplicators. The man had surrounded himself with a large army of predatory Arab horsemen and a great number of richly dressed slaves who served coffee and sherbet to those waiting to see the great man.

A number of lions, suitably chained, was a clear indication that Zobeir claimed royal privilege, and he was but one of a number of major challengers. Zobeir had left his son Suleiman in charge while he travelled to Cairo to negotiate with the Khedive. However, to strengthen Gordon's hand, the Khedive put Zobeir under house arrest, a move that was to have considerable consequences.

And finally, of course, there was money. What a curse money was! Why had it ever been invented? In the past princes had been able to live off the riches of their lands without being bothered constantly by Treasury matters. Gordon had much sympathy for Ismail when he spoke in this vein. At last the Khedive finished and waited for Gordon to reply. Gordon's description of what followed was brief to the point of terseness, but perhaps it tells us all we need to know.

'Then I began and told him all, and then he gave me the Sudan—and I leave on Saturday morning.'

Ismail said with some trepidation: 'The salary of the Governor-General is £6,000 a year.' Gordon said that it should be £3,000. Ismail did not argue the matter, at £3,000 it was fixed. Ismail knew that the huge bribes that were by custom paid to a governor-general would never be taken by Gordon. Gordon would either refuse them or pay them into the Khedive's Treasury. Which he did was left to Gordon. As it turned out Gordon adopted the latter plan. The administration needed the money and the bribes had become so established that they represented an indirect but effective form of taxation.

Ismail insisted on his tailors making for Gordon a sumptuous uniform in gold and purple with the royal insignia embroidered into the collar. It cost £150, a large sum at this time, but even Gordon admitted it was worth it. 'It certainly does impress the sheiks,' he said later.

Before he left Cairo Gordon persuaded Ismail to issue a firman officially appointing him Governor-General of the Sudan, with Dafour and Equatoria thrown in. He was to have three deputies: one in Khartoum where Gordon would reside in the vast new palace, one for Dafour where Suleiman, the son of Zobeir, might be expected to be troublesome, and one for the Red Sea Hills that included the little trading-post of Port Sudan, the only outlet to the sea that the Sudan had as an effective port of call. Ismail Yacoub was removed from office and his family, in Khartoum, resented this greatly. His sister even ripped the rich silks of the Palace to pieces before the family left, and Ismail Yacoub and his friends were to be enemies of Gordon to the end. The Khedive's proclamation of Gordon's appointment was a tribute to the faith he had in him. Gordon was charged with the improvement of communications, and the suppression of slavery and 'disorder', and at the special request of Mr Vivian the English Consul-General these words were added to the firman:

'*Il y a sur la frontière d'Abyssinie des disputes; je vous charge de les arranger.*'

These were the kind of terms of reference that Gordon appreciated. In effect Gordon was to do the job as he thought fit.

On this occasion Gordon did not clash with Sir Evelyn Baring (afterwards Lord Cromer), who had recently become England's representative in Cairo, but this did not prevent Gordon forming an unfavourable impression of Sir Evelyn. Gordon mentions in a letter that Baring was of Dutch, probably Jewish, extraction and 'closely allied by family ties to powerful European finance'.

In fact the Baring family were German Jews of high standing and integrity. But Baring represented everything that Gordon distrusted. The handsome, urbane, conservative figure who now loomed large in Cairo as Britain's voice in Egypt stood in Gordon's eyes for the new class of merchants and bankers who appeared to be taking over in England, ousting the aristocracy and old families like the Gordons who had long Service traditions. Money, Gordon felt, was very important to Baring. Gordon, as we know, had no time for it. Precedent was a desideratum that Baring greatly liked. To Gordon the fact that a thing had been done in a certain way for a number of years was no recommendation. Baring was essentially a man of the desk and the filed report. He liked to have everything in writing. Gordon was always inclined to play his cards by the light of Gordon, which, in his more sententious moments, he would regard as almost divinely inspired. The clash between the two men was inevitable. In Baring's world there was no room for unpredictable genius. In Gordon's world there was room for little else.

Gordon knew that Baring would suspect and distrust his friend Ismail, the Khedive, and Gordon thought, not without reason, that Baring would have great sympathy with the Khedive's European creditors. Debt was anathema to Baring. It was untidy and probably dishonest. To Gordon, with his distrust, amounting to dislike, of money the question whether one owed it or was owed it was of secondary importance. What was important was men's freedom, their peace, and their happiness.

In the years that lay ahead Gordon was unable to circumvent Baring. Baring was too powerful and too trusted to be by-passed.

Gordon could reach London, officially, only through Baring. This was to irritate him more and more, but it is fair to say that Baring, according to his rather dimmed lights, was much fairer to Gordon than Gordon ever was to Baring. It was a classic clash of two irreconcilable temperaments.

Gordon decided to deal with the Abyssinian dispute first before going to take up his duties in Khartoum. He sailed down the Red Sea to Massawa and from there settled the border disputes to his satisfaction, playing off one chief against the other in the best British tradition of 'divide and rule'. He had the choice of making an alliance with Johannes and allowing him to swallow the border provinces, but he chose instead to support Walad El Michel and built up a belt of semi-independent border provinces which might prevent, or at least delay, any conquering ambitions that Johannes might be harbouring against the Khedive. His task accomplished, he mounted his camel and set out through the provinces of the Red Sea Hills for Khartoum.

Gordon had now to put up with any amount of ceremony and protocol. He was 'His Excellency the Governor-General' and, as was the custom in the Khedive's domains, greatness was surrounded with a horde of yes-men and servants. Even in Massawa Gordon had a foretaste of what was to come. His dinner-table at night was laid for twenty persons. Gold plate was provided and three black eunuchs stood immobile behind the chair of the great man. When he mounted his camel ten servants hastened to help him and there was a similar rush of willing hands when he dismounted. If he wanted to walk everyone in the retinue had to walk too, and petitioners, who were very numerous, approached him at the crawl, kissing his boots and feet. Gordon genuinely disliked all this very much, though with pleasing vanity he was rather attached to the magnificent uniform the Khedive had ordered for him. It made him look almost handsome.

One result of Gordon's visit to Massawa that he may perhaps have foreseen was that the people of Khartoum were kept on tenterhooks as to when Gordon was actually going to appear.

Rumour was as rife and as ripe in Khartoum then as it is now; and every kind of rumour percolated through the town about the coming of Gordon. The family of the deposed Governor-General spread a rumour, hopefully, that he had been murdered by tribesmen, but no one really believed this, even those who would have liked to have done so.

So numerous were the petitions on the way to Khartoum, when it was discovered that the Governor-General would listen to every complaint, that a post-box had to be set up at each camp into which petitions could be dropped. They were sorted out by secretaries early in the morning and then Gordon himself would deal with them, giving his brief decisions with despatch, but as impartially and fairly as he could on his knowledge of the facts.

Gordon never gave up this habit of availability. It was, of course, in the best tradition both of African and Arabian monarchy. But it had been dropped by the great officers of the Khedive who were always too busy torturing, or being pampered by their concubines, or feasting, if they were not devising new means of extortion. To the people on Gordon's route the fact that this man, who was the friend and trusted servant of the Khedive, should deign to listen to all their grievances was almost a miracle. The practice over the years gave Gordon a real place in the affections of the people and probably accounted for the fact that Gordon never lacked informants and spies who were prepared to tell him everything.

On the 3rd of May 1877 it was reported in Khartoum that Gordon was on his way, only a few hours' march from the city. Then as now Khartoum is an oasis in the desert, which comes right up to the city. An hour's ride from the city Gordon's considerable cavalcade, headed by the green flag of Islam and the Khedive and the personal banner of the Governor-General, was still crossing open desert. It was not until they were within a few minutes of the city that the mirages stopped playing their tricks and the mosques of Khartoum itself loomed up on the horizon. Very soon it was possible for Gordon to dismount his camel and travel into the centre of the city, in the Governor-General's barge, along the Nile.

People lined the banks in their thousands. When the barge was sighted a whisper that grew in volume as it sprang from one multitude to another, from the river-bank to the market, from the market to the residential quarters, from the houses to the barracks and up to the Palace itself, told every soul that Gordon was here— at last.

He stepped ashore in his grand new uniform, a regal little figure. The guns fired their salutes. The addresses of welcome were read and then a silence that could be heard fell on the crowd, for they were eager to know what kind of reply he would make.

It was usual on these occasions for the dignitary to make a long reply, expressing his sense of mission, warning those who might dare to oppose him, and praising those who had served the Khedive as well.

Gordon decided that he would make a very brief speech, in fact a speech of eleven words. Perhaps because it was so short they would remember it.

Raising his voice he said:

'With the help of God I will hold the balance level.'

When they heard these words a shout went up from the people, for this was what, more than anything else, they were hoping for. They had been exploited pitilessly by Ismail Yacoub and his family.

Taxation was appalling. The prisons were full. Justice was a farce. Bribery was the accepted custom of all official transactions. If, indeed, the new Governor-General was going to curb their exploitation then the people of Khartoum, especially the poor and the oppressed, were on the side of Gordon and would do anything he asked.

The innumerable windows of the Palace were ablaze that

night. The damage that had been done by the vindictive family of the former governor had been repaired. The great rooms glistened and shined, and it was midnight before Gordon reached the sanctuary of his bedroom that contained a four-poster bed of imperial proportions. The servants would not leave him alone, but insisted on undressing him and then massaging him and bathing him with warm, scented water. In the end he managed to get rid of the last retainer. He could hear the guards still chattering outside his door as they roamed the passages. Then all was quiet. A half-moon had risen over the Nile and Gordon went to the window to look again at the great river as it shone in the light of the moon.

There was a portrait of the Khedive opposite his bed; he looked aloof and regal, not as Gordon knew him.

Gordon put out the light and kneeling, as was his habit, said his prayers. To himself he repeated what he had said to the people of Khartoum: 'With the help of God I will keep the balance level.'

Sleep came quickly and peacefully. The mission had started. Gordon now controlled the destinies of the ten million people in the million square miles of the Sudan.

14

Full Moon

ONLY the northern coast of Africa had been known for centuries
to Europe. The Roman Empire, including Carthage, had stretched
for hundreds of miles along the Mediterranean shore. Even the
African animals, the hippopotami and the elephant, were known
in Rome and shipped there for labour or for zoos. But the body of
Africa remained a mystery. Islam spread over what the Romans
had held and extended the area, but still it left the interior mainly
uncharted, unmapped, unknown.

The Portuguese were the first great power to tackle the
African interior, and their empire in Africa extended along the
east coast for a thousand miles and included Angola, Loanda,
and Benguela. Typically the Portuguese boundaries in the interior
were not defined. They were set as far as the effective writ of the
Government in Lisbon would run. The Portuguese set a pattern
of African government which was simple and ruthless. Its aim
was the exploitation of these vast areas for the enrichment of
Portugal. Slave labour and service contract labour were essential,
it seemed, to achieve that purpose.

It is possible that if Sir Samuel Baker had been successful
in his mission, the British occupation of the Sudan, which was to
come much later, might have followed a similar pattern, but in
fact a different approach to Africa, from a very early date, was
established. The British in India had been so successful because
they had stuck to two rules. The first was divide and rule with

impartial fairness. The second was to leave the indigenous trade partly in the hands of the Indians, who were in this way encouraged to co-operate with the British firms and so, indirectly, the British Government. The fact that it was Gordon who took Baker's place also had a profound effect on the course of events. Gordon was proud of the dynamic, aggressive British 'discovery' of Africa. Stanley and Livingstone, he thought, had blazed a trail that was a challenge to the adventurous spirit abroad in Britain. Other great powers, of course, would try to get a slice of the cake, but it was the British, with their great knowledge of native administration and rule, who were destined to play the major role.

There is no accounting for the sense of complete self confidence that in any age may grip a people and a nation and cause them to think of themselves—and even be accepted by others—as the lords of creation. Britain was such a nation in 1874. It was not arguable, Gordon thought. The more power and influence Britain exerted, the better it would be for everyone. It meant that these backward people would, in the not too distant future, receive the benefits of roads, railways, the telegraph, and the opportunity to adopt a Christian way of life, if not Christianity.

Gordon's unique gift was that he was genuinely interested and concerned for the happiness and rights of the Africans as well as for the general upsurge of British power everywhere. And, of course, he was in the Khedive's service. Turkey might be becoming the sick man of Europe, but the empire of the Sultan was still vast. Egypt represented, because of its periodic independence, by far the most enlightened portion of this empire. No one could pretend that the Egyptians, though they might have their faults, were not a civilized people. The Egyptian upper class was sophisticated, cultured, and spoke French fluently. So that Gordon's sense of mission for England, which he always remembered in times of difficulty and anguish, was always tempered by the fact that he was in the Khedive's service. His uniform was the uniform of Egypt, not of Britain. His salary was paid from the Cairo Treasury, and the ultimate orders that he could not ignore came from the Khedive.

These factors and his own firm faith and Christian outlook

made Gordon the ideal man to be Governor-General of the Sudan. The Sudanese were—and are—a mixed race. At Wadi Halfa, on the Egyptian border, many of the types appear indistinguishable from the Egyptian in feature, even in expression. The semitic Moslem man dominates as far as Khartoum and even beyond, but, together with these aquiline people with their lighter skins, there are the African negroes, and the two types intermingled. To the north the country is Islamic and Arab. To the south African and pagan. Gordon had the peculiar gift of being able to get on with both strains in the Sudanese. He seems to have had no race prejudice at all. This was not so uncommon in the 1870's as it became later. The old Queen was saying that 'there is no distinction in our minds between a white skin and a brown—none'. Yet there is a certain amount of evidence that race-and-colour prejudice was introduced into our Indian Empire by the *memsahib*, a lady often elevated from comparatively humble circumstances in Britain to one of considerable pomp in India, but capable, nevertheless, of sexual jealousy and inspired by a ruthless determination to maintain British privilege in its convenient glory. The *memsahib* never really got her teeth into the Sudan. It was too vast—and the climate was abominable. The pattern of race fraternity that Gordon was to set remained, and still exists.

In London there was a broad division of approach to Africa. The Conservative Party and the City, at that time perhaps not so strongly linked as at present, joined in demanding a bold, 'forward-looking' policy that would not miss a trick in this exciting new game of African poker, in which the stakes were so high. The Liberal administration on the other hand were set against military adventure. The British Empire, they thought, was quite big enough already. What was important was the development of British trade in all the newly emerging territories. They did not accept the contention that trade, invariably, followed the flag. By and large they favoured peaceful penetration.

The British public, who seem to have had a genuine affection for Gordon from the start, appear to have thought that Gordon reflected what was best in both these ideals. He was liberal, but he was Christian; he was a soldier, but he was an administrator.

State war-drum of the Mahdi

Spears and war-drum of the
Dervishes

'The Camel Rider', formerly at Khartoum, now at Gordon's Boys' School, Woking

(*Below*) The restored tomb of the Mahdi photographed by the author from the Khalifa's house

He was British, but he had a cosmopolitan vision. The quirks in Gordon's character did not worry them at all. If it was true that Gordon, when he asked for guidance from God, invariably obtained the answer that he wanted, an answer that would sustain and increase the influence and power of Gordon himself, they were not surprised. It showed only that Gordon and his Maker were attuned one to the other. We must accept it that a degree of what we, today, might call hypocrisy was acceptable as an ingredient of life by the Victorians. Their convictions were more absolute than ours. Their profound belief in their race, their language, their mission, and their Queen, made sceptical questioning appear irrelevant. The emphasis was on admiration, not denigration. All great men, no doubt, had in them something of the charlatan, but that was an ingredient of their greatness, not a defect of their character.

Because these were their attitudes and this was their thinking, Gordon, as Governor-General in Khartoum, was always at the back of the minds of people in Britain. They were proud and delighted to have him there. They did not mind that he represented the Khedive and not the Queen. That only showed the adaptability and flexibility of British policy. He was an Englishman, and he was in command. That was sufficient.

Hardly had the firman been read by the Cadi and the royal salute fired than Gordon, installed in his vast palace, began to reform the Sudan with a spate of directives such as the Sudan had never experienced before—or since. There were a hundred abuses to be remedied and the best time for doing so, according to Gordon, was always 'today, not tomorrow'.

Taxation on the farmers was crushing. It must be lightened at once. Usurers must be controlled. The prisons were filthy and the prison administration in the hands of officers who relied almost entirely on flogging to keep discipline. These floggings, inflicted with cowhide whips laced with lead, were so severe that the victims often died. If they did not they were broken men, and were willing to crawl in submission until the day of their release, a date that was never divulged to them. These men, the victims of brutality, without hope, soon found their lot bettered. Floggings were forbidden. Sentences were confirmed to the prisoners.

I

Even they, together with every other man in the Sudan, could petition the Governor-General if they could have their supplication slipped into that box at the Palace that was available, night and day, for petitions. The really wicked elements in the Army and police and even in the priesthood were weeded out and retired, with or without a pension or gratuity, according to their records. Then they were either despatched to Cairo or retired in the Sudan.

The effect of Gordon on Khartoum was electric. This little man, a trim alert figure with his red fez and white uniform, accompanied by his guard and his secretaries, was busy from morning till nightfall. He woke at dawn and after a frugal breakfast he started the day's work, working till sunset. Then he would change into a loose-fitting Arab-type costume of cotton and retire with his tobacco-jar and his glass of brandy to the palace roof to look over the city and ponder. He could see the Nile from here, and the great bends in the river, one to the north round which the steamers from civilization came, and one to the south which led to the interior and ultimately to the Great Lakes. This hour of respite was all he allowed himself. Then he had to change into uniform again and go through the protocol of dinner and perhaps, afterwards, a reception.

Dinner was a gigantic affair. Hares and antelope, Nile perch—an excellent eating fish—and every type of sweetmeat loaded the table. The fruits were very varied and included olives, oranges, figs, sweet melons, water-melons, pomegranates, and ju-jubes. There was no way to cut short this feast. Gordon was as much a prisoner of convention as the Queen was at Windsor. The receptions he did manage to shorten, sometimes by passing his hand in a dramatic gesture over his brow, a gesture that indicated that the Governor-General was fatigued. The pashas and the sheiks invariably took the hint.

Gordon's training as an engineer enabled him to extend the primitive water system of Khartoum, and soon water was available at the houses at no great cost. These were the kind of projects nearest his heart. But the Palace, with its two hundred rooms, had no great appeal for him. He missed the camel-rides, and the adventures of his governorship of Equatoria. It was not very

long before he found an excellent excuse for leaving the capital
and taking to the country. Suleiman, the son of the formidable
Zobeir, was giving great trouble in Dafour.

Gordon had already perfected a system of espionage radiating
from Khartoum and he was extremely well informed as to what
was going on in the provinces. He received information that
Suleiman, angered by the fact that the Khedive, reportedly at
Gordon's request, had imprisoned his father while he was the
Khedive's guest—a flagrant breach of hospitality in Suleiman's
eyes—was on the rampage. Although only in the early twenties,
the young man felt that he must now take his father's place and
he had gathered a huge collection of ivory, which Gordon had
proclaimed a government monopoly, as well as an army of over
seven thousand men and a like number of slaves. This was
rebellion on the grand scale. The spies further reported that
Suleiman was marching on Dara with the intention of taking that
town and enlarging both his empire and his loot.

This was the kind of challenge that Gordon could not resist
and, speedily making his preparations, he set out with the troops
he could spare and a personal guard of two hundred men such as
was customary for a governor-general.

Suleiman and his brigands had pitched their tents near Dara
and Gordon, having far outstripped his escort, arrived in that
town alone. He had been lucky enough to secure an exceptional
camel for the last stage of the journey, an animal that liked to be
given its head so that 'its padded feet seemed to skim the surface
of even the roughest terrain'. On one occasion on this ride this
camel had shaken off its nose-ring and carried Gordon at a
terrifying speed, which the rider could neither curb nor halt. A
little black boy who ran suddenly into its path was almost killed,
but escaped by a miracle.

The people of Dara were stunned at seeing the Governor-
General ride in alone. Gordon was a living legend in the Sudan
by now, but no one expected to see him unannounced. Gordon
made full use of the shock of these tactics. He acted before the
people had time to recover from their stupefaction. He determined
to strike at Suleiman before that young man knew what had hit
him.

He slept in Dara, was too fatigued to eat dinner, and at dawn he got up. In a letter he describes what happened:

'I got up and put on the golden armour the Khedive gave me. Then I went to see my troops and mounted my horse and with a band of *my* robbers I set out for the camp of Suleiman, about three miles distant. I rode to the chief tent in the camp. The chiefs sat there dumbfounded at my coming among them. I accepted a glass of water and told the son of Zobeir that he should report to me at my Divan. He and his family came and, in my best Arabic, I explained that I knew through reliable information that I had just received that they were premeditating revolt and must now accept my ultimatum, namely that they should surrender their arms, their ivory, and their slaves, and break up.

'They left, and shortly after I received a letter from Suleiman accepting my terms. I thank God for this.'

Suleiman, taken off guard by the boldness and swiftness of Gordon's moves, and knowing that his father was still in the hands of the Khedive, had surrendered, but with honour. He expected Gordon, as was customary when allegiance was given, to present him with robes and he also asked for a governorship. Gordon refused, saying that the young man had not yet given any sign that he was either contrite or loyal. Yet it is clear that Gordon had genuine sympathy for Suleiman. 'I hope', he wrote, 'that the son of Zobeir does not hate me too much for my harshness to him.'

As if these formidable enterprises were not enough to keep Gordon occupied, about this time he lost his secretary who Gordon discovered had accepted over £3,000 in backsheesh. Gordon at once sent him for trial in Khartoum. Berzato Bey, a well-educated young Moslem, took his place. 'He has,' said Gordon, 'the distinction, a valuable one, of saying when he disagrees with me.' Gordon had constant difficulty in securing reliable deputies. No doubt the material available was partly to blame, but Gordon contributed to it, for he was apt to regard all his new brooms as swans at first and then when they turned out to be no more than human to cast them out as geese.

Gordon, on his appointment as Governor-General, had been made a pasha of the Porte and the cry, 'The Pasha is coming!'

was enough to strike terror into the hearts of all those who knew that their activities might incur the displeasure of the Governor-General. But his prestige alone was not enough to account for his success. There were two other factors. The first was the speed with which he travelled. So terrifying was the pace he set himself that camels died under him. When this happened he changed, without apparent thought, to a new mount. The second quality that subdued potential rebels was his courage. He did not seem for a moment to realize the appalling dangers of the situations in which he placed himself.

When Gordon returned to Khartoum a full moon was lighting up the waters of the Nile. It was a full moon too in the career of Gordon Pasha. The Khedive in Cairo sent him a message of encouragement and appreciation. The Sudan, in town and in the desert, was quiet for a while—but it was the lull before the storm that was to come like a dust-cloud out of the desert, sweeping all before it.

15

'Slavery Must be Smashed'

As usual, when the Governor-General had been absent from the capital for a time, work had piled up in Khartoum. Gordon tore into it the day after his return. The papers, many of them petitions, each presented its own problem. The facts of each, often complicated, had to be mastered before a decision could be reached or judgment given. Gordon developed the knack of the lawyer in busy practice for assimilating with accuracy one set of facts, deciding on the real issue and discarding those facts so that he could take in the next case. He worked with meticulous care, but with great rapidity.

In the late afternoon, when the sun relented a little in Khartoum, he liked to roam the city, looking in unexpectedly at a prison or inspecting one of his irrigation projects. His progress was always hindered by the crowd who followed him wherever he went and kept up an incessant shout of supplication. Most of them were petitioners who felt that only the Governor-General himself should decide their case. Gordon's attempts from time to time to delegate his work never met with success. The people believed that only he would give them a fair deal, and for this belief they had their reasons.

He had not been in Khartoum long before he felt, as he put it, 'the call of my camel'. Although he complained that his heart, his liver, and his lungs had all been shaken out of position by his constant camel-rides, he loved this mode of transport. He loved the freedom of the desert. There were no roads to constrain one. A journey meant following the caravan tracks or branching out over the sand, taking one's bearings by the White Nile or the Blue Nile, by the sea or by the stars. At night the tents would be put up, the fires lit, the sentries posted. It was infinitely remote. This was government at first hand, Gordon thought. Here I am, the travelling authority of the Khedive, settling matters as I find them, seeing with my own eyes, hearing with my own ears, giving judgment on the spot with nothing between me and my petitioners.

In these circumstances the real genius of the man was able to assert itself, and Gordon himself, at this peak of his power, formed a good impression of his own capabilities.

He decided that it was time he visited Walad El Michel again and the sail to Berber gave him a period of forced idleness and the rest he sorely needed. 'The quiet of the day on board the steamer going down the Nile is quite delightful,' he writes.

He is happy: 'I have a great contentment. A star when it reaches its highest point is said to have culminated, and I feel I have done this. . . .' He refers to Isaiah, taking the prophecy as his own:

' "And it shall be for a sign and for a witness unto the Lord of Hosts in the Land of Egypt, for they shall cry unto the Lord because of the oppressors, and he shall send them a Saviour and a great one, and he shall deliver them." '

Gordon in this mood was apt to place himself on the right hand of God whom, indeed, he refers to on one occasion as 'my Governor-General'. This strain of religious fanaticism never left him. Always, in the fashion of the day, he was apt to identify the wishes of the Almighty and his own immediate plans. Yet from the very deepness of his conviction that his mission was divinely supported he drew his strength, his indefatigable energy, and his supreme self-confidence.

At Berber and Dongola he found a mountain of complaints against the governors who had been up to their old tricks of extortion and corruption. He dealt with the petitions as best he could, but he could not stay long and a crowd followed him out into the desert when he left, crying out to Allah that their wrongs were still unrighted. He despaired of reaching Walad El Michel, for the Khedive was sending him telegrams to return to Cairo for 'urgent consultations'.

He ignored these and pressed on, crossing two mountain ranges and encountering a manifestation of flies that brought a new horror into life, for they would settle on the camel's head like a black, moving mask. However, he did reach Walad's camp and, to all appearances, was made prisoner in some humble outhouses which had a high stockade. Walad was said to be 'unwell', but Gordon sent him a stern note that if the authorities in Khartoum did not hear that the Governor-General was safe they would at once telegraph the Khedive who would punish those concerned 'without mercy'. This was no idle threat. The methods of the Khedive when dealing with rebels and traitors whom he decided not to spare for possible conversion were bloodcurdling, and included the slow pulling to pieces of the victims and the rubbing of salt and acid into the wounds caused by this mutilation.

Walad took the hint, and next day was all apologies and ready to talk. Gordon again resisted the temptation to hand Walad over to Johannes and he arranged the frontier once more within the terms of that generous mandate that had been written into his orders at the request of the British Consul-General. Gordon did not believe he had secured peace on the Abyssinian border. 'I have patched the matter up,' he said.

The Khedive's telegrams could be ignored no longer and Gordon steamed down to Cairo to arrive very late one evening at the Palace, unchanged and unshaven. The Khedive, he was told, had waited for him an hour and a half, but was now dining. Gordon joined the banquet. He was surprised and touched by the fact that Ismail had kept a vacant chair for him on his right hand. What was it the Khedive wanted? Something, obviously, was in the air. He was lodged in Kasrel Kousa that night. This was the Guest Palace used only for visiting royalty. Waited on by fifty servants Gordon felt suffocated, and wished he was out under the stars again.

Next day in audience with the Khedive he listened while Ismail explained his plan. Gordon was to be chairman of this new Finance Enquiry that the European creditors insisted on setting up. The terms of reference were to discover what was the public income of Egypt. What were the debts? How could the nation be put on its feet again? The position was very serious.

Gordon had to agree to undertake this work, for which by nature and by training he was most ill suited. Gordon secretly shared the Khedive's distrust and dislike of money. 'It was,' said the Khedive, 'a botheration.' But the Khedive knew that Gordon was his friend and would fight his battle in committee. This Gordon did, but he hated the work. He had an acrimonious quarrel with Sir Evelyn Baring who most unwisely regarded himself as Gordon's superior. He suspected that he was 'being made use of'. And he just could not understand the extremely complicated facts and figures that were laid before him. Even the Khedive had to admit that the appointment was not a success. To ask a man who did not believe in money to settle the finances of Egypt was asking too much. 'I miss my camel,' Gordon told the Khedive and, before long, the Khedive reluctantly let him go back to his governor-generalship and the work he understood so well.

It was then that Gordon made his last supreme effort in the Sudan, an effort directed at carrying out one of the major duties with which he had been charged—the complete suppression of slavery. He decided that Suleiman in Dafour was the arch-culprit. The Khedive would do nothing about Zobeir, the father. He lived comfortably enough in a Cairo villa on the £100 a month allowed him by the Sultan. He was in the Khedive's power, but the Khedive would take no steps against him. Suleiman interpreted this as a sign of weakness, and an assurance that whatever he did his father would not suffer.

Some steps Gordon could take in Khartoum. They were administrative, and aimed at making life more difficult for the slavers of Dafour. All persons residing in Dafour had to have a *permis de sejour* and all persons entering or leaving Dafour a passport.

All slaves from the south-west on the road to the Sudan and Nubia had to pass through Dafour. On paper at any rate these measures would have strangled the traffic at the bottle-neck. Yet appalling accounts of the extent of the traffic reached Gordon.

Fifty thousand deaths a year. Over a hundred thousand slaves held in fiendish conditions. Gordon decided to go to war. He had given Suleiman every chance. Personally he liked the tall, handsome young man. But he had broken his word not once but many times. He was in danger of becoming more powerful than his father Zobeir had been. As long as he lived slavery in Dafour would flourish, for Suleiman's riches and Suleiman's power rested on ivory and slaves, and, of the two, slavery was by far the richest source of revenue. Suleiman when confronted with Gordon himself had given in. He had sworn fidelity and allegiance. But as soon as Gordon's back was turned he hardened his heart, and reverted to his dynastic ambitions and his relentless pursuit of slavery without mercy.

Gordon was in a dilemma as to what he could do, legally, to the slavers. There was a firman that said that slaving was punishable by imprisonment. There was the spoken word of the Khedive who had said to Gordon: 'Shoot them, if necessary.' And there was a letter from Nubar Pasha that asserted 'the purchase and sale of slaves' is legal in Egypt. Nevertheless, Gordon decided to act and to act swiftly.

Having made up his mind he marched on Sharka and sent Gessi with seven hundred well-armed men to chase Suleiman. On the road to Sharka Gordon came across slavery in all its horror. Nothing that had been printed in London by the Anti-Slavery Society[1] could equal the stark horror of slavery as Gordon saw it. Between June 1878 and March 1879 Gordon accounted for nearly seventy caravans. Not expecting him, the slavers' cavalcade would be trundling across the desert and Gordon would swoop. Ten or more caravans with outriders would be followed by a line of slaves several hundred yards long, the men yoked like oxen with wooden girdles round their necks, the children often tied to the chains that linked one group of slaves to the next.

If a man failed on the march from exhaustion he was lashed by the guards until he continued or dropped. If he dropped he was thrown to the side of the track and the ever-hovering vultures

---

[1] The Society, with offices in London, is still active, attempting to counter the remnants of slavery, mainly through the United Nations Organization.

would descend on him, as he was dying, before the caravans were out of sight. The slaves would take the lesson to heart. They had either to march or be picked to pieces, their flesh torn to ribbons by the ghastly hopping scavengers that followed the slavers like a black cloud.

When Gordon rode in and freed the slaves they were over-joyed but helpless. They could only crawl and supplicate. Many could not stand. They had lost their manhood. They would cringe at the sight of a raised hand or a whip. They were as abject as ill-treated animals. 'I cry for them,' Gordon wrote, 'but all I can do is to free them.'

Meanwhile Gessi, as brave and resolute as ever, was pursuing Suleiman. Often in the months that followed Gessi was in great danger. Suleiman's forces outnumbered Gessi's by at least four to one, but Gordon had told Gessi Suleiman would break under constant attack, and Gessi carried out the instructions of his chief. At last Gessi cornered Suleiman, catching up with him by a last forced march of incredible speed.

At the village of Gara, at dawn, Gessi struck while Suleiman's men, believing that Gessi was at least a day's march away, slept. Gessi, who already had achieved a minor victory over Suleiman's troops, struck, setting fire to the huts and sending his men, who were now flushed with victory, in to kill the alarmed camp. Suleiman was captured and on orders from Gordon shot with his chief lieutenant. The man who aspired to be the unquestioned King of Dafour was dead, meeting a rebel's end, his head being exhibited as a warning to others.

Gordon made Gessi a pasha, gave him a money grant, and arranged with him the future government of the Bahr Gazelle. It was a victory of real importance. The only real threat, at present, to the authority of the Khedive had been crushed. Gordon pursued his advantage, stationing troops at the wells throughout the district. Water the caravans had to have or die, so to the wells they came where Gordon's men would meet them, free the slaves, and imprison the slavers. It really looked as if slavery in the Sudan was going to be stamped out for good.

Gordon attempted one more great diplomatic coup as

Governor-General. It became obvious that the policy of bolster-
ing the border kings and 'containing' Johannes of Abyssinia was
not working. That monarch, suspecting he was feared by the
Khedive, was becoming daily more aggressive. His original
modest demands on Egypt had now swollen prodigiously and
Gordon, at the request of Cairo, decided to beard the King of
Kings in his den.

It was a risky undertaking. The journey itself presented every
kind of difficulty, from fever to brigands. Gordon, who travelled
with an escort of a hundred men, was in constant danger of being
attacked while his men slept. He had long given up being surprised
when Egyptian sentries slept at their post. His energy and
enthusiasm that, during the past two years, had been so high,
were running down again, and he was apt to accept behaviour
that only a few months previously would have enraged him.

He was received at the court of Johannes with a salute of
guns, but the following day, when in audience with the King, it
was clear that the King was in a very unbending, proud mood. A
stool had been placed for Gordon far below the divan occupied
by the King. Gordon knew exactly what this meant, and he
immediately moved the stool and placed it alongside the divan.
The King made no comment at first, but after they had taken
coffee he said: 'Do you know, General Gordon, that I could have
you killed?'

Gordon was not put out. He replied that he was ready for
death any time. That his religious beliefs prevented him from
taking his own life, but that death at the hands of another would
in many ways be a merciful release. He would avoid whatever
trouble might lie ahead.

This extraordinary reply seems to have disturbed the King,
for he made no more threats but proceeded to advance the most
outrageous claims againt Egypt. Gordon said at once that Bogos
could not be ceded, but Zeila was another matter. The King rose
abruptly, saying that he would put his reply to the Khedive's
letter in writing and hand it to Gordon next day.

The answer that Gordon did receive was suspiciously brief,
and when Gordon had it translated it was insulting.

'I have received your letter by that man. I will not make a

secret peace with you. If you want peace ask the Sultans of Europe.'

Gordon suspected that the Greek Consul, who was very close to the King, had been at the back of the King's decision to press for terms that he knew would not be granted. Gordon set out to return, his mission a failure.

As Gordon was leaving Abyssinian soil he was suddenly arrested by Ras Arya, the King's father, and not released for some days. Altogether Gordon's impression of the Lion of Judah and his people was an unhappy one. On them his spell appeared to have little effect. He was tired perhaps, and when fatigue overtook him his magnetism waned as if it was sparked by an exhausted battery.

In Khartoum bad news awaited him. Ismail, getting deeper and deeper into debt, after one final plunge that lasted six months, during which he dismissed his European advisers, had finally been dethroned himself by the Sultan of Turkey who had risen from his couch to make this last great gesture of authority over his Egyptian Empire. Ismail's son, Tewfik, was put in his place, but Tewfik was a pale shadow of his father.

Ismail cleaned out the Treasury before he left, taking some millions with him in his yacht the *Mahrousa*, and finding a refuge in a palace in the Bosphorus where he was able to enjoy his wine and his concubines in peace.

Gordon travelled to Cairo, this time to resign for good. He had no mind to serve under Tewfik, whom Gordon suspected of being a puppet of the foreign creditors of Egypt.

In Cairo he had furious and undignified rows with Nubar Pasha and some other ministers. The new Khedive accepted his resignation with grace, but without too much regret. It seemed that the days of Gordon Pasha were over. In the best Egyptian tradition the new Khedive would have his own friends, his own favourites. On the way home Gordon managed to quarrel with Lord Lyons, the British Ambassador in Paris, saying that if Britain did not send a good man to the Sudan he, Gordon, would ask the French to do so. And, when the Ambassador was put out, Gordon merely said: 'Never mind, a little box coffin will soon be all that either of us will need.' The only explanation of this extraordinary incident appears to be that Gordon thought the Ambassador pompous and that he was being naughty. He never indulged in these tricks when he was well and rested, but now he was tired and dispirited.

Soon after reaching London even sadder news awaited him. Gessi had died in Khartoum after a disastrous expedition. Gordon was heartbroken for he loved Gessi and had trusted him more than any of the men who had worked with him in the Sudan.

'Gessi! Gessi! Gessi!' he wrote to his sister. 'I warned him to leave me, but his life was bound up with mine.'

Gordon returned to London and this time he would not speak of the Sudan. Nothing, he said, would induce him to return. He was ready to do any job that did not entail government and great decisions. He wanted desperately to be rid of the Gordon of legend.

For a spell he had his way. He embarked on a number of missions which, compared with his work as Governor-General, were trifling, but then, unknown to Gordon, in Cairo a Colonel Arabi—an Egyptian patriot—was to storm to power; and in a small island one hundred and fifty miles upstream from Khartoum a man was to appear who proclaimed himself a Mahdi and his mission a Jihad or Holy War.

These two men swung the course of Egyptian history into a new path that threatened both the Khedive and Britain; and Britain, in desperation, and in the most perilous circumstances, was to turn, for the last time, to Gordon for leadership and salvation.

16

Who Wants Gordon?

GORDON's retirement from the Sudan, which appeared at the
time to be final, offered him the opportunity for rest. He was
entitled to leave in any case—leave and leisure. He did manage
to spend a few weeks without working, mainly in London and
Southampton. Without working, but not without a certain amount
of activity. He wrote letters to the Press, sometimes under his
own name, but usually using a pen-name on questions affecting
the Sudan and Africa as a whole. One has the impression that the
seventies and the eighties were the heyday of the 'letter to *The
Times*'. Everyone read these letters. The more obscure the
signature the greater the speculation as to who the forthright
author might be. In the small oligarchy that then ruled England
and the Empire, in which all the major families and figures knew
one another, *The Times* correspondence column was as much a
forum of public debate as the House of Commons itself. Gordon
visited the offices of the Anti-Slavery Society, at that time very
active. So he spent his weeks of leisure ruminating, thinking,
his brain always active, his spirit never quite quiescent.

Determined attempts were made to lionize him, again. But
Gordon adopted the most peculiar means of dodging the duchesses.
He would reply in the name of a secretary that Colonel Gordon
had left town abruptly without leaving a forwarding address.
He would say he had a touch of the old complaint, 'Sudan fever',
and ask to be excused. He would say anything rather than go.

He even refused an invitation to dinner with the Prince of Wales. The Prince's equerry who had been entrusted with the personal delivery of the invitation to Gordon—apparently the Prince knew of Gordon's little ways—was distraught. 'But, Colonel Gordon, I must give some reason.'

'Tell him I always go to bed at nine-thirty.'

Eventually Gordon's reluctance was overcome. It was hinted to him that to insist in his refusal would upset the Queen. Gordon capitulated at once. There is no record of what passed between the worldly, shrewd Prince with the guttural German accent and Gordon, but there is no doubt that the Prince satisfied his mother's curiosity as to the kind of man Colonel Gordon really was. From this time on the Queen followed the fortunes of Gordon with personal interest. She believed in him and his missions absolutely.

Early in May Lord Ripon, the new Viceroy of India, was choosing his staff. He asked Gordon to be his private secretary. To the amazement of the public and the Press Gordon accepted. He regretted this decision almost immediately. But Gordon sailed with Lord Ripon and took up his duties on the voyage.

The Press in London and in India buzzed with speculation. Why had Gordon really accepted a post that required all the qualities which even his friends admitted he had not got? A viceroy's secretary had to be a man of fashion, a man urbane, understanding, and skilled in the niceties of protocol and of society. Gordon was no such man. The British Empire in India was now reaching the height of its glory. The Viceroy was in fact an emperor—communication between Delhi and London was too slow for home decisions to be made on urgent questions. The Viceroys lived in very great state, keeping a court sustained by a splendour and a pageantry never before surpassed in Asia.

What was Gordon doing in all this grandeur? The speculators hit on several explanations, the most plausible being that he had been sent secretly to adjust and agree the border with Afghanistan and Russia, which was assuming the proportions of an open and ominous dispute. How clever of the Government to get Gordon to India to accomplish this task, for which he was supremely well suited, so quietly and so appropriately!

Alas, nothing so clever had even been attempted. Gordon

resigned as soon as the Viceroy's ship reached Bombay. He stated that he had had no dispute with Lord Ripon, who had been more than kind to him, but that he had regretted his acceptance of the post almost at once, but had not had the moral courage to say so. What it was that brought Gordon's dislike of his new post to a head we shall never know, but we may perhaps conjecture that, during the long weeks of the voyage, Gordon got an inkling into the kind of nepotism and jealousy that surrounded a viceroy and the petty intrigues of the ladies around the throne to improve their position. If this was the reason his resignation was not in the least surprising. Something deep in Gordon's character warned him that women spelt danger, and his instinct was to steer clear of them if he could. The Sudan had been very much a man's country and, apart from the love he had for his sister, Gordon strove to keep the complication of women out of his life. Perhaps they made him feel inadequate. In any case they represented a challenge that he did not accept.

Gordon was again without a job, or at least in the process of reverting to his regimental duties, if such a reversion were now possible. Colonel Gordon, it may be, had become too great a figure to be contained for very long in the strait-jacket of regimental life. The seven years at Gravesend were to be the last long period in which it was possible for him to be a serving officer again. Out of the blue came a telegram from his old friend Li-Hung-Chang, inviting him to China. The message was contained in a telegram and couched, as one might expect, in the most gracious and pleasing terms. China, on the point it seemed of engaging in hostilities with the Russian Empire, needed Gordon.

Gordon could never resist this kind of appeal, and at once obtained leave to sail for Hong Kong where he stayed with Sir John Hennessy at Government House and rested for a few days in their lovely garden, ablaze with flowers, on the Peak. Then he travelled to Canton and met Li. The two men, who had been through so much together, wept when they saw each other again. Li was a very great man now. He had the peacock's feather, the yellow jacket, the post of Senior Guardian to the Heir Apparent. But his mandarin's mask fell away when he saw Gordon, and he ran over to hug his friend and say that it was like old times again.

K

There was at this time a pro-war party in China led by Prince Chun and Tso, a soldier-statesman. Li, whose ally was still Prince Kung, was working for peace. Gordon backed Li from the start. Gordon was asked to prepare a report on the 're-organization' of the Army and the strategy to be pursued. This he did and it is a remarkable document, for it showed a mode of thought at least fifty years ahead of its time in respect of China. Gordon started off in his report by telling the Chinese to do it themselves. 'You need no great European officers,' he said, 'to accomplish what has to be done. If I were to direct it it would only stir up jealousy among the other foreign governments. Nor need you alter the pattern of the Chinese Army, which is traditional and suits the people.'

Having said this he went on to advise in great detail how the Emperor's army could be most effectively and economically used. The gist of his recommendations was that the forces should always be employed as guerillas, making use of their intimate knowledge of the terrain to harass an enemy night and day without ever engaging in a major action or even, for that matter, being seen. Thus the Chinese losses would be very small, but the enemy would never have an hour without anxiety. The vast area of China could be used to make these tactics effective. An enemy might capture a city but the very roads by which he had approached it would by that time be in Chinese hands again, certainly at night, and even, if it paid the Chinese, in daylight hours as well.

The whole report is a fascinating study of warfare in the guerilla, commando manner, assuming many of the techniques that were forgotten in World War I and only rather reluctantly resorted to in World War II. Underlying all Gordon's advice was Churchill's axiom that you must, if you could, hit without being hit.

Gordon, the engineer, goes very carefully into what China should have by way of weapons. 'The soldiers travel very light,' he says. 'This is their great advantage. They eat off the country and are very mobile.' They should carry only, he advised, a simple, sturdy breech-loading rifle, effective up to a thousand yards. Gordon was dead against heavy artillery. He was against the storming of cities—a rule which he had not always obeyed himself. He favoured the Chinese always buying time by yielding ground, but always coming back. There is no doubt that these tactics could have swallowed and rendered impotent a huge foreign force in China. The Russians knew how to give ground and conquer. It is perhaps just as well for them that they never attempted a wholesale invasion of China after Gordon's report, which was translated by the Press and, pursued by the Government, had become effective Chinese policy. Gordon was equally frank about army pay and discipline and the opening up of the country by the extension of the telegraph and the use of sun-signals by the heliograph. As to the defence of the coast, here he advised against the emplacement of static, heavy, and expensive guns, and in favour of heavy mortars. Great numbers of these could be purchased and they would make a foreign invasion a hazardous undertaking. The Chinese fleet should be light, fast, and capable of operating in shallow water, in the creeks as well as the open sea.

This was an extraordinary report for a British officer of the day to write. It shows that Gordon was tackling the problem as if he were a Chinese. He was looking at it through Chinese eyes, trying to fathom only what was best for China. He ended his report by saying:

'If I stayed in China it would be bad for China. China can do what I recommend. If she cannot I could do no good.'

Gordon has never quite been forgotten in China. Even today, in spite of new ideologies, he is remembered.

He returned to London in 1881. As yet there was no post available for him. He crossed over to Belgium to discuss with King Leopold a Congo expedition which the King wanted Gordon to lead. Gordon always had the idea at the back of his mind that if the forces in Whitehall that tried to keep him back became too powerful he might enter the service of the Belgian monarch. He saw nothing strange in this. European divisions were not so marked and tense at this time. The struggle in Africa, as Gordon saw it, was the Christian ideal as opposed to the Moslem way of life. But whatever plans Gordon had in mind were ended, for he was appointed Officer Commanding Royal Engineers in Mauritius. In Mauritius he spent ten quiet, uneventful months carrying out his duties. It was the last short period of service for Colonel Gordon, the regular soldier.

In April 1882 the Government of the Cape asked for his services. Gordon secured permission to accept their invitation to end the grave position and fighting in Basutoland. This mission was probably the one single failure of Gordon's career, and for this his nature was only in small part to blame. The Cape Government acted most unwisely and in bad faith. It was also unfortunate that after the invitation had been sent the Cape Cabinet changed.

Gordon understood his position as being one of a negotiator and administrator. He was to settle the war, bring the rival kings Letsea and Masupha together, and restore peace. No doubt he might have accomplished this. Following his old tactics he did beard Masupha in his court and returned alive to the amazement of the Cape politicians. But the new Cabinet gave him grudging support. He was, they insisted, only to be the commander of the colonial troops under direct orders from Cape Town. This Gordon could not tolerate.

It was, he felt, a breach of the terms on which he had undertaken the work. He resigned, his mission unaccomplished. The Cape Cabinet were not too sorry to be rid of so autocratic an adviser.

In the spring of 1882 he was back in London and there is no doubt that, at this period of his career, Gordon was regarded at the War Office as a man of remarkable talents who had no sense of private—or public—relations whatever. They made him a major-general, but no post was made available for him. The time had come, it was suggested, when General Gordon might like to take things more easily, to retire in fact.

This he did not do, but he did take advantage of his enforced idleness to make a dream he had harboured for many years come true. He went to the Holy Land and took a house on the outskirts of Jerusalem. 'I want to stay in bed till eleven,' he said, 'and have oysters for lunch.' This sybaritic dream was not to shape the pattern of his life. No sooner was he settled in than he became intensely interested in the Holy Places of Christianity. Living on unleavened bread and dates, and cutting down his consumption of tobacco, he started to study the sites of the tabernacle, the sepulchre, the walls of the city, and the details of Nazareth and Jericho as well.

He had the flair of the engineer for excavation and exploration and he said that with a map in his hand and the country under his feet, with the Bible references available, he could find the actual location of all the greatest sites. He drew complicated but meticulously accurate charts, which are preserved to this day, and it did not really surprise anyone who knew Gordon that the sites Gordon had found to be authentic were not the immemorial sites of Christianity.

Gordon's discoveries and theories were taken seriously and they upset the Churches. It really was very inconvenient after nearly two thousand years to be told that the Holy Places were all in the wrong place. Gordon produced proof of his theories, and it is a tribute to his ingenuity that his drawings and conclusions are still the subject of heated argument.

Peaceful academic disputes in the Holy Land were not to be Gordon's destiny. New trouble, real trouble, had come swiftly in the Sudan. After one major victory, that made Britain virtually the ruler of Egypt, Britain had suffered a humiliating defeat, for she had lent a Colonel Hicks to lead an expedition against this new menace, the Mahdi. True, the troops had been Egyptian, but British prestige had suffered its direst blow when the Mahdi destroyed the Hicks army by slaughtering it in a sudden, overwhelming attack.

What was to happen? It looked as if a great pan-African revolt was in the making. It looked as if all those dreams of Britain and the Khedive were to be shattered in a Moslem revolt of such ferocity that no European would be able to stay in Africa. The vast new continent that had beckoned the Great Powers with riches in ivory and slaves and gold was on the point, it seemed, of going up in flames.

This was a major conflict. Great interests as well as prestige were involved. Britain was not prepared to be driven out of Africa. Her civilizing mission, her great expeditions, her investments, and her zeal for empire were all at stake.

In this situation the cry went up in the London press: Where is Gordon? Hiding away in the Holy Land.

Then he must be brought back. He must be given *carte blanche*. No niggling restrictions must be imposed on him. It must no longer be pretended that here was an ordinary serving British officer. He had, this man, the unalterable, mystic signs of greatness that could not be defined, but could be recognized.

Gordon returned, reluctantly, to London, but before we follow him on his last adventure we must know in more detail what had been happening in Egypt and in the Sudan while he had been discovering new sites for old. And in particular we must meet the man who now called himself the Mahdi—a religious fanatic, or patriot, or both—who was causing such perturbation in Whitehall that the rulers of Britain were prepared to turn once more to Gordon.

17

The Mahdi

As long as Ismail had been Khedive and Gordon his viceroy in the Sudan the strong currents that always flow beneath the surface of Egyptian and Sudanese politics had been kept in control. Ismail may not have been ideal as a ruler but he understood his people. He was adept at playing off one powerful pasha against another, and, in spite of his urge for modernity, his people never doubted that he loved his country and was working for her good. His personal extravagances were dwarfed by his public extravagances. At least there was something to show for all the money, and Egypt appeared to be marching towards a new and better future. Moreover, Ismail never appeared to be in the hands of foreigners. To the end he would keep the British and French representatives waiting while he attended to other business. To the end he was the Khedive in fact as well as in name.

Ismail had a keen appreciation of merit in others, especially those qualities of forthright loyalty and courage which, sometimes, his ministers appeared to lack. In choosing Gordon as his Governor-General in the Sudan he assured not only peace in that vast area, but the potential growth of his empire. The shadow of these two men stretched out over Egypt and over the Sudan so that no man dare challenge their authority on a grand scale.

This was the position until Ismail was deposed and Tewfik was made Khedive. When Gordon also left, the whole picture changed. The Khedive was openly seen to be in the hands of the

British and French representatives in Cairo who stood for the foreign creditors. In the all-important matter of money Tewfik could not pretend that he was master in his own house. If there was a payment on interest from the Treasury it was not Tewfik who decided how much it should be. If there was a moratorium its terms were dictated—foreign terms. And in Khartoum the new governor-generals appeared to be vacillating, subservient figures after Gordon. Sedition and revolt no longer feared swift retribution.

In order to understand what followed we have to appreciate the Egyptian character, and the likely manifestations of Islam when confronted by the encroachment of a foreign ideology. While Gordon was upsetting the patriarchs in Jerusalem by pointing out to them that most of the Holy Places should be moved to new sites, the cauldron was coming to the boil both in Cairo and in Khartoum.

In Cairo a body of young Egyptian officers led by Ahmed Arabi were plotting revolt, a revolt aimed at throwing the foreigners into the sea and proclaiming the sovereign independence of Egypt. The Egyptians are a clever, ambitious people, subtle and civilized. Always, it seemed, subject to some kind of foreign pressure or domination, they burningly desired freedom. Their nature provoked a passionate pursuit of any ideas that were put before them with complete conviction, and Arabi was at least as sincere as President Nasser who, urged by the same ideals, has become a power in our own time.

Arabi was not a great man, but he was a fine, handsome figure of complete integrity. He was the kind of man the Egyptian crowd, always a factor in Cairo politics, would follow blindly. On the 8th of September 1881 Arabi and his men, who with their regiments had been ordered out of Cairo, struck, marching on the Abdin Palace and making Tewfik a virtual prisoner. The Khedive capitulated at once. Perhaps he was not too reluctant, for though a weak man he must have felt his humiliation at the hands of the foreigners. Here at last was violent, direct protest. The rebels had no intention of killing Tewfik. Having agreed not to interefere with the revolution he was permitted to take up residence in another palace on the outskirts of Cairo. From there,

surrounded by his unique collection of *objets d'art* and his faithful courtiers, he watched the explosive developments of the next
weeks rather as he might have watched a play at his new Opera
House.

Both the British and French governments demanded the
resignation of the Arabi regime, but there was nothing that
Tewfik could do about it even if he had wanted to. Arabi set up
a dictatorship under the nominal patronage of the Khedive.
Attempts were made to restore order, but by now the mob were
more violent than their leaders. Europeans everywhere were
insulted and spat upon. Crowds roamed the streets not only in
Cairo but also in Alexandria. Sir Charles Cookson, the British
Consul, lost his trousers and was injured when pursued by an
angry mob. The act seemed to symbolize the insult as well as the
damage to Britain. Mr Gladstone, who believed that any British
intervention would mean the end of Anglo-French co-operation
in Egypt and commit Britain to far-reaching military and administrative liabilities, fought against war, but to no avail. Public
opinion was stronger than the Government.

The British adopted the tactics that had proved effective
before. A British fleet under Admiral Seymour appeared at dawn
off Alexandria, demanding the dismantling of the Egyptian shore
batteries. When this was not at once complied with a large number
of British subjects were taken aboard the ships and the city was
bombarded. It took some time and the fleet suffered some direct
hits, but the batteries were silenced.

The mob was in delirium. This was war. These were the
infidels. The mobs took over in Cairo and Alexandria and some
hundreds of people were injured, many being killed. In some cases
at least the old Islamic custom of dividing the offending infidel,
one section of the mob departing with one leg, another with the
other, was adopted. But if the mob was guilty of atrocity so was
the British Army which, under the command of Sir Garnet
Wolseley, was landed to bring Arabi to battle.

The battle of Tel-el-Kebir was the first decisive battle of the
Nile Valley in this era. The second was Omdurman. In both the
slaughter of the enemy by the British troops was a gigantic carnage.
For the loss of less than fifty men the British commander witnessed

the killing of over four thousand men of Arabi's army and the pursuit of the remainder, who were cut down as they tried desperately to escape the vengeance of the British. Arabi reached Cairo and was sentenced to death, but by now the British had cooled off, reverting to their normal diplomatic ingenuity. Arabi was exiled to Cyprus in the best tradition of modern British colonial diplomacy.

Gladstone, the irritating old man, was right, of course. Anglo-French relations reached a very low point. The French, still powerful in a largely French-speaking Egypt, devoted themselves to disrupting and undermining British influence and prestige in Cairo. They did not meet with the success that their industry appeared to merit, but their government did take Tunis, and this act of open aggression brought them the renewed suspicion and dislike not only of the Egyptians but of all the Moslem people.[1] It was not until twenty years later that the British and the French signed a treaty defining their relative spheres in North Africa.

Moreover, Gladstone was right in saying that if the Arabi revolt was crushed Britain would be committed not only to ruling Egypt but also to ruling the Sudan. As it turned out the Sudan could not at this time be ruled by anyone, for in that country a rising far more ominous than anything that Arabi had thought of was under way, led by a strange figure whose command over his followers was inspired not by military discipline but by fervent religious faith.

The British public heard for the first time of a man who called himself the Mahdi.

The Mahdi was presented to the British people as a religious fanatic, a description that invariably aroused the deepest suspicion in Britain where it was the custom to be coolly devout. The Press made fun of this 'desert fakir', who had proclaimed himself a liberator and the chosen of the Prophet, the designated leader in a Jihad or Holy War. But it was not for long that the British press and the cartoonists were able to laugh, for in a very short time it was clear that the Mahdi represented some elemental

---

[1] Even at this time there was a feeling of brotherhood between the Islamic states.

force in Islam that threatened to sweep all before it. Soon he took on the appearance of a terrifying figure.

In fact Mohamet Achmet, a native of Dongola, the new messiah, was a man of singularly imposing presence and fine bold features. Those who met him for the first time remarked upon his smile, that seemed for ever to hover on his lips and was of great sweetness. The smile hid from casual observers a relentless will and a flair for religious and political leadership that amounted to genius.

So Egypt had surrendered to the infidels. Should the people of the Sudan do the same? The answer that the Mahdi gave was a resounding *no*. And that answer was backed by thousands who were prepared instantly to die for him and count it their greatest blessing. This was fanatical, but it was a quality that the Egyptian troops in the Sudan certainly did not have. It made the Mahdi and his followers a power that was to challenge Christianity and the foreign penetration of the Nile Valley by inflicting the most appalling series of military defeats on Britain that she has ever had to endure in a comparatively short space of time.

The Mahdi at this time was handsome, in his late thirties, a figure who inspired absolute devotion. Wherever he went men knelt to kiss the hem of his garment. His word was law. Later, corrupted by the flesh, the Mahdi was to become a gross figure, donning his patched *jibbah* only when he had to face the multitude, pampered, scented, seduced by his women in private, but never, to the end, did he lose his grip on the imagination and loyalty of his followers. In the beginning, these numbered only a few hundreds, but, like a gathering dust-storm from the desert that grows ever larger, darker, and more menacing, the Mahdi's followers multiplied until he was leading thousands, many of whom were trained horsemen and desert fighters.

The first news that the outside world had that a new force had arisen in the Nile Valley was in midsummer 1882 when it was learned that every man of a six-thousand-man force under Youssuf Pasha sent to quell the Mahdi had been routed and slaughtered by the Mahdi's dervishes. This was bad enough. Obviously the Mahdi must be taught a lesson. A Colonel Hicks was put in command of a large force of over ten thousand men with orders to bring back the Mahdi in chains. Colonel Hicks met with initial success, but the Mahdi retreated towards El Obeid, crossing the desert with a swiftness that Hicks's men could not emulate. Hicks decided to pursue the Mahdi and then suddenly, on the 3rd of November 1883, a screaming multitude of dervishes fell on Hicks's ungainly column. They were wiped out.

The consternation in Cairo and in London was unprecedented. It looked as if all Islam might be in flames and that this detestable man, who only weeks before had been regarded as a figure of fun, was going to play a major part in the destiny of Africa.

Worse news was to follow. Six hundred Egyptian troops marching from Suakin to Tokar were fallen upon and hacked to pieces.

At Trinkitat Baker Pasha suffered a humiliating defeat, losing, it was estimated, two thousand five hundred men for less than a thousand enemy losses. These fiascos were to some extent retrieved by the partial victories of Sir Gerald Graham against the rebel leader Osman Dinga, but the forces of revolt in the Sudan were nowhere quelled and in many districts they ruled in undisputed sovereignty.

The British Army was now serving in Egypt—the Black Watch, the Gordon Highlanders, the 10th and 19th Hussars, the 60th Rifles, and the Marines were all there on active service. Yet against the sudden ferocity of the Mahdi's men it was impossible to establish British rule. Constant reports came in to Cairo that one isolated garrison after another had been stormed and destroyed. At Sincat the garrison had eaten horseflesh for days before they attempted to break out, only to be cut to pieces. The news got progressively worse.

The Mahdi was developing illusions of grandeur now. He was reported as having advised Queen Victoria to take the faith of Islam while there was still time. Whether anyone had the temerity to pass on this message to the widow of Windsor history does not record. But the British press were as one in demanding the recall of the one man whom, it was thought, could work the miracle and bring back peace to the turbulent deserts of Upper Egypt.

Gordon must be sent out. He could not refuse. He had never

refused to serve his country. Britain, smarting under the humiliation of her defeats, turned to Gordon. His name alone inspired confidence. Gordon spelt success in whatever he undertook.

But Mr Gladstone was reluctant to send Gordon out under any conditions. He had insisted that the Khedive should pull his garrisons out of the Sudan, back to Wadi Halfa which was regarded as the border of Egypt itself. Tewfik agreed but with bad grace, for this was admitting defeat.

Then a new situation arose. It was all very well to say: Evacuate the garrisons and the foreign communities. But could they any longer be evacuated? The Mahdi's friends, it was said, were encamped on the banks of the Nile between Khartoum and the border. No matter; Gordon could no doubt accomplish what was desired. But how to get round Gladstone? Lord Granville thought he knew just how that could be accomplished. Gordon could be sent not as Governor-General or as military commander but merely as a reporter and—perhaps—a negotiator. The position might be desperate, but the magic of Gordon's name would work wonders. He might even win over the Mahdi.

After some weeks of delay the Prime Minister consented. It was a fateful decision for Britain, for Egypt—and for General Gordon.

18

Gordon Returns

THE decision to send Gordon on a mission to Khartoum was not easily arrived at. Mr Gladstone, the Prime Minister, was at first resolutely opposed to it. But some of his powerful ministers, Lord Granville the Foreign Secretary, and Lord Hartington the Minister of War, who could better be described as Whigs than as Liberals, were smarting under the disasters of recent months, the Hicks tragedy in particular. In taking this attitude they were only voicing popular opinion. The man in the street felt that something must be done and done quickly. The man in the street was, however, still inarticulate. There was no great Trades Union movement through which he could voice his political beliefs.

The Times, as usual, was in the forefront of the debate. On New Year's Day 1884 Sir Samuel Baker, still regarded as an authority on Egypt and the Sudan, wrote a letter to the editor suggesting that a strong military force under General Gordon should be sent to restore order in the Sudan. Action now, said Baker, would avoid chaos and possible tragedy later. It was a sensible, forthright letter. It evoked great support.

Then W. T. Stead, perhaps the greatest journalist of his day, interviewed Gordon at Southampton. What did General Gordon think about it all? The readers of the *Pall Mall Gazette* would like to know.

The readers of the *Gazette* were left in no doubt as to what General Gordon's views were. The time to act was now. The

Mahdi represented a real danger only if allowed to grow bigger and stronger unmolested. He must be brought to heel at once. The man to do that? General Gordon suggested Sir Samuel Baker, whose strong-arm methods in the Sudan were vividly recalled. Gordon himself was not available. He was on the point of leaving for the Congo. The King of the Belgians had not 'given' the Congo to Gordon, but he had offered Gordon a post which, with Gordon's flair for enlarging his sphere of influence, would probably turn out to be that of viceroy with plenary powers.

So Gordon was suggesting Baker, and Baker was proposing Gordon, as the man of destiny.

They met very quietly in Devon at Baker's house in Sandford Orleigh. Gordon made the journey to Newton Abbot by train, and one is reminded of Sherlock Holmes making the same familiar journey to look into the strange affair of the Hound of the Baskervilles.

Baker did not really want to play a hero's part any longer. He preferred to live peacefully in Devon and to vary the soporific routine of life in Devon by an occasional letter to *The Times* that always commanded respectful attention. He started to work on Gordon. Gordon should give up all thought of the Congo. At least for the present. King Leopold would wait. The Sudan was much more urgent. Gordon, and only Gordon, could bring peace and security back to that troubled country. Baker did not explain how this was to be done. It would have been superfluous. Already Gordon, his eyes shining, was advancing one idea after another. Sir Samuel Baker had 'sold' the Sudan to Gordon.

There was still one snag and it was a serious one. Sir Evelyn Baring in Cairo, who really did know what was going on throughout the Khedive's domains, if they could be called that any longer, objected to a Gordon mission in the most strenuous terms. The Government in Whitehall said that all they desired was to pull out of the Sudan. Could Gordon be trusted to adhere to such terms of reference? Baring thought not. Gordon was not the kind of man who willingly pulled out of any challenge. He was much more likely, Baring thought, to turn round as soon as he reached Khartoum and insist that the real remedy was to smash the Mahdi—and that meant war.

Baring's protest held matters up for some days. Gladstone knew that Baring was too big a man to allow his personal dislike of Gordon to form his judgment. He genuinely believed that Gordon's nature was such that he could not be trusted to carry out a mandate of surrender. But the Government was now being swept along by an irresistible current of clamorous public opinion. Fleet Street was for once almost united. Gordon must go. The experts were unanimous. Gordon was the only hope, and by this time Gordon himself obviously believed that he could accomplish more in the Sudan than any other man. Perhaps the Press, the experts, and Gordon were all right.

Gordon was summoned to a Cabinet meeting and the Foreign Secretary, presiding in the absence of the Prime Minister, who was indisposed, stated the Government's terms. 'We are determined to evacuate the Sudan, for we cannot guarantee its future government.'

This meant that Tewfik was to be forced to agree to withdraw all his garrisons from Khartoum and elsewhere, and that the Government washed their hands of the Sudan. This was General Gordon's mission. Did he accept the terms? Yes, he accepted.

Gordon's mandate left one great, sinister, unexplained question-mark to fate. If the garrisons could be evacuated was the Sudan to be left a vacuum? The Mahdi's men did not yet control the towns. They were still desert armies waiting and watching, striking with ferocity and cunning if attacked, swooping on small garrisons that they knew they could overcome, but by no means in control of the administration.

In spite of the doubtful loyalty of the tribes on the banks of the Nile above Wadi Halfa the Mahdi's men were still confined to two great centres: El Obeid, where the Mahdi ruled unchecked, and the Red Sea Hills, where Osman Dinga was powerful and predatory, a constant menace to the link that joined Suakin and the Red Sea coast to Khartoum by camel-track.

No attempt was made to tackle the question which this position really posed. Presumably the Sudan was, in effect, to be given up to the Mahdi, but neither Gordon, nor the Cabinet, nor the sedulous correspondents of *The Times*, faced up to this issue. It was blurred by the magic of Gordon's name. When Gordon was in Khartoum everything would change—for the better. It was a policy of appeasement, of course, or perhaps of surrender, but with Gordon to execute it it would not seem like that. Gordon was capable of winning over the Mahdi. He would make one of his strenuous lightning camel-rides and appear in the Mahdi's camp armed only with his character and his cane, and the Mahdi would be talked into co-operation. The Mahdi might even be made a governor, given a title, and become loyal to the Khedive and, indirectly, to the Queen of England. But the Mahdi was not that kind of man.

Gordon was seen off by the Foreign Secretary and by the Duke of Cambridge who afterwards reported to the Queen personally on the scene. From this moment on one is aware that the old lady who ruled England is watching Gordon's progress with sympathy and ever-increasing anxiety. She made her ladies-in-waiting read her every reference—and there were many—to General Gordon in the months ahead.

Characteristically, Gordon had forgotten to take any money with him and the party who had come to see him off pressed banknotes into his hand. The Press reported the incident with relish. A Colonel Stewart joined Gordon as his second-in-command. Colonel Stewart was sent with Gordon partly to assist him, partly to keep an eye on him. He was regarded as a very reliable officer with no nonsense about him. This was Gladstone's concession to Baring's view that Gordon needed watching. So the Light and Shadow of the Light departed, with the good wishes of all England and the prayers of many.

Gordon travelled across Europe by train and at Brindisi took the S.S. *Tanjore* to Egypt. On the ship he had some enforced days of idleness. The more inactive he was physically the more his brain worked, and a hundred schemes flitted through his fertile mind, some of substance to be developed later, some to be dismissed as soon as he had considered them.

He sent a telegram—the first of hundreds—to Baring saying that they had better have Zobeir watched. If he vanished from Cairo and linked up with the Mahdi a very dangerous situation might arise. Could he not be shipped to Cyprus? As Zobeir was technically the guest of Tewfik, as he had been of Ismail,

L

Baring did not feel he could arrest him and deport him, but he did have Zobeir's bungalow watched night and day. If Zobeir had harboured any idea of joining the Mahdi he was no longer able to do so.

Gordon wished to sail down to Suakin and do his old trip of crossing the Red Sea Hills to Khartoum by camel. How nice it would be to ride a camel again and get away from all these ministers with their written instructions and their inhibitions! It would enable him to avoid Baring, too, who probably wanted to impress on Gordon how restricted his mandate was. And Tewfik of course—though what Tewfik thought was becoming less and less important. It was not the old Cairo that Gordon had operated in with Ismail and Nubar Pasha. Baring was a very great man now, a dominating figure. Baring effectively countered these plans by sending a telegram to Port Said instructing Gordon to report to Cairo. Gordon could not disobey. Besides, it might be that he could enlarge his powers in Cairo before he started on his mission, and receive valuable funds as well. As it turned out he could do both.

It was as well that Gordon did not attempt to reach Khartoum from Suakin, for Osman Dinga, still very much alive, was waiting to pounce on any travellers through the Red Sea Hills that he did not approve of and, had Gordon attempted the journey, he would in all probability have either been put to death by Dinga or sent in chains as a prisoner to the Mahdi. So Baring saved Gordon from possible disaster at the start of his mission. The incident goes to show how little Gordon understood the changes that had taken place in the four years since he had quit the Sudan, and to what extent he under-estimated the strength of the Mahdi's movement. Gordon was, at this stage, dangerously over-confident.

Gordon got on much better with Baring this time. Baring was the completely loyal civil servant. The Government had over-ruled him. They had decided to send Gordon out to do his best. Baring at once gave Gordon all the support he could, but he did take the rather doubtful precaution of asking Colonel Stewart to report to him privately. It was not a request that Gordon would have approved of, and it was not a request that looked very good.

But in politics and diplomacy one has to play the cards as they come, and ethics are made to fit into convenience.

However, he made considerable progress. He had an audience with Tewfik and said how sorry he was that in the heat of the moment, when leaving Cairo, he had made some derogatory remarks about His Highness. Tewfik smiled and held out his hand.

Gordon was set on taking Zobeir with him to Khartoum to play Zobeir off against the Mahdi. Zobeir had real influence with the sheiks. Yes, yes, he had of course been a great slaver, but that was best forgotten. He could be very useful now. The administration in Whitehall dreaded agreeing to Zobeir's reinstatement. England, they thought, not without reason, would be horrified at using a man whose name in Britain stood for slavery, torture, and cruel absolutism. But even these fears and scruples could probably have been overcome by gentle, insinuating persuasion that the rulers of Britain knew so well how to handle. It was Zobeir himself who upset the plan. He refused to shake hands with Gordon. Gordon had put his son Suleiman to death. After a stormy interview the idea of Zobeir travelling to Khartoum was abandoned. One likes Zobeir the better for this. He might well have reached Khartoum and had his revenge on Gordon by stirring up the tribes to join the Mahdi. His passion overruled him. The old man still mourned his son.

Before he left, Gordon did have a major victory. He persuaded Tewfik and Baring to agree to him being made Governor-General again. And he received £100,000 to carry out his mission with the promise of more if he needed it. What had happened to the reporter who was to supervise the evacuation of the garrisons? He had melted away a little. The Governor-General had taken his place. But still his position was defined in two firmans: the first announced the reappointment of Major-General Gordon as Governor-General of all the Sudan; while the second, which was not published and was only to be made public at Gordon's discretion, announced the intention of withdrawing the Egyptian garrisons from the Sudan. Colonel Stewart watched the metamorphosis of his chief with interest but without surprise. He was getting to know Gordon.

As Zobeir had refused to co-operate with Gordon, the Emir Abdul-Shakour, who belonged to the house of the hereditary princes of Dafour, was chosen to accompany Gordon. It was thought he might be very useful. Gordon was already perturbed by the thought of the vacuum that he would leave behind him if he was able to evacuate the Egyptians. The idea of setting up the hereditary sheiks and restoring their powers was very much in his mind, and it was for this reason that the Emir—who was accompanied by a gigantic retinue of servants and wives—was taken as a travelling companion for the Governor-General. However, Gordon quarrelled with the Emir, a touchy man, and he was left behind at Assuan. He did in the end penetrate into the Sudan, but on his own he had no plan of action and was soon back in Egypt and no longer a factor in the clash between Gordon and the Mahdi.

Gordon rested for some days at Berber to make a declaration to the local sheiks whose loyalty was said to be wavering. He deliberated for some time as to what he should say. At last he made up his mind that the proper course was to reveal the contents of the Khedive's second firman which stated that it was the intention of the Egyptian Government to evacuate the Sudan. Gordon enlarged on this considerably by saying that power was to be restored to the local rulers—who were his audience—and that the slave trade would henceforth be regarded as legal.

What induced Gordon to say this, even in the circumstances he found himself in, it is difficult to say. It seems to run counter to his character. The only comment appears to be that Gordon, like the rest of us, was not always the same man. The sheiks listened in silence and left, apparently satisfied. But in fact they were deeply disturbed. Did this mean that the Mahdi was winning? It might well mean that. Why else should Gordon Pasha give the slave trade his blessing—however reluctantly—why should the Khedive feel that he had to evacuate his whole army? If things were as desperate as that it might be a good idea to join the Mahdi before it was too late. The Mahdi was not being conciliatory to anyone. He was taking up the position of a conqueror whom none dare oppose, and it was widely known that, if he were opposed, the Mahdi was not a gentle man. On the

18th of February 1884 Gordon and his party reached Khartoum, and were received by the officials and the population with a genuine demonstration of loyalty and affection. In Khartoum, at any rate, Gordon's name was still magic, and heartened by his reception Gordon was able to cast his spell once more over the city.

The last few days on the river had given Gordon ample time for thought. As usual, his spirits rose when he was on the move and out of range of officialdom. The river itself still had a message for him, a message of strength, courage, hope. The man who landed opposite the Palace that had been prepared for him was Gordon the Governor-General, with all his authority and determination.

Gordon set up a Council of Notables to assist the Governor-General. He destroyed the instruments of torture in the prisons and sent Colonel Stewart to see that the debtors in gaol were set free. The gates of the city were flung open and a declaration was posted that anyone who wished to go and join the Mahdi might do so. Very few availed themselves of the opportunity, fearing perhaps to reveal their hand.

The Mahdi made no move towards Khartoum. He was, as we now know, puzzled and not a little afraid. He thought that Gordon must have support at hand or that major forces must be moving to his aid either from Egypt or from the Red Sea Hills. The prestige of Gordon's name was such that the Mahdi revolt froze, but the menace was still there.

Gordon, now much reassured, contemplated his maps and considered the situation. He evacuated a few Egyptian troops and then sent a telegram to Baring saying that it would be a mistake to denude Khartoum of its garrison, for 'Mahdism must be smashed'. Just as five years before it was slavery that had to be smashed so now it was the Mahdi.

Baring was deeply perturbed at this line of argument. It cut right across the agreed policy both of Her Majesty's Government and of the Khedive. But Gordon kept up his barrage of telegrams. He switched to trying to get Baring to persuade Zobeir to come up and play the part that Gordon had in mind for him. Baring tried hard to arrange this, but Gordon, too precipitate, gave the story to *The Times* correspondent in Khartoum, a Mr Power. The story broke in London and such was the outcry that the Government had to drop Zobeir once and for all.

February had, however, on the whole been a good month for Gordon. His good reception, his first swift acts of order and clemency, his obvious authority, were reflected in the opinion, in London, Cairo, and Khartoum, that Gordon was going to bring it off. The Mahdi would be checkmated if not routed. The heat came in March, the wicked, arid heat as the temperature rose to 120° and over. On the thirteenth there was bad news that came out of the blue. The tribes to the north had revolted. They had cut the telegraph line to Cairo. Khartoum was isolated. Though Gordon did not immediately realize it, the siege of Khartoum had begun.

19

The Siege of Khartoum

ANYONE who has been a prisoner for a long period knows something of the frustration and the fears that a siege entails. Abnormality is commonplace. Small incidents become grotesquely enlarged. The courage, by which alone man lives, is weakened or strengthened by the hope of relief and release.

Khartoum was besieged for three hundred and twenty days from the 13th of March 1884, when it was learned that the tribes to the north had joined the Mahdi, to the 26th of January 1885, when the Mahdi's dervishes finally summoned up enough daring to storm across the shrunken waters of the river into Khartoum itself.

Relief arrived three days late. Between September and January almost any relief force would have turned the Mahdi away from Khartoum. Gordon said that two hundred trained troops would have been quite sufficient, not of course to defeat the Mahdi, but to deflect him. Nearly eighty years later the appalling disgrace of the failure to relieve Khartoum still discredits for all time the Cabinet of Mr Gladstone, who vacillated and lied rather than act. The Queen was stricken by the Cabinet's behaviour. Setting aside all convention that she should not interfere in affairs of State she wrote boldly to her Prime Minister: 'Gordon must be trusted and supported. What he asked for repeatedly nearly five weeks ago has been refused. If only for humanity's sake, for the honour of the Government and nation, he must not be abandoned.'

The Cabinet under pressure attempted to deceive both the Queen and the House of Commons. The House was told on the 21st of April by the Prime Minister in person that 'as far as we know Khartoum is not besieged'. The Queen was assured that steps were being taken that would draw valuable information from General Gordon. This was cowardly political chicanery at its worst level. The Government must have suspected, if they did not know, that Khartoum was already surrounded. They knew that communications between Cairo and Khartoum had been 'interrupted'. They must have drawn the inevitable conclusion that Gordon was in great danger, but it was not until the 16th of August 1884 that Lord Wolseley arrived in Cairo to take command of the relief expedition. They had four months to reach Khartoum, sixteen hundred miles to the south, and so dilatory and cumbersome was the movement of the force when it did eventually get under way that even that period of time was not sufficient. Up to September the politicians had wasted six months. After September the military command consumed four months before they reached their objective. Had there been a national enquiry into the disaster Mr Gladstone and his immediate colleagues would have been the first persons to be charged with dereliction of duty, but certainly, after them, Lord Wolseley and his commanders would have had to take a share of the blame.

The military failure rested on the complete misunderstanding of the situation. When Gordon got a message through by river that he could hold out for six weeks the reaction was that, if Gordon said he could last six weeks, he could certainly survive six months. It was madly, sickeningly, illogical. Lord Wolseley appears to have had in mind only the final crushing of the forces of the Mahdi, a large-scale battle in which the new Maxim guns would mow down the dervishes in the manner that was in fact achieved, thirteen years later, at Omdurman.

But this conception was wholly false. His mission was to relieve Gordon. The relief of Gordon did not entail the smashing of the Mahdi. It entailed only pushing up the Nile as rapidly as possible with a token force that could be constantly reinforced as further flying columns arrived. The Mahdi had real fear of the British soldier who, in the eyes of the dervishes, was a ruthless butcher armed with weapons no man could resist. He did not fear the Egyptians. He knew their lines would break before the blood-curdling cries of a dervish spear-attack. It is clear now that the Mahdi, up to the end, was always ready to retreat towards El Obeid if help arrived for Gordon, whatever form the help might take. It was only when he was presented with Omdurman and Khartoum by the prolonged inaction of the British Government and High Command that he decided that, to his surprise, Gordon was at his mercy. It was almost too good to believe, but circumstances gave the Mahdi the opportunity to learn the truth at the time that Gordon's spies were regaling him with false or faulty information.

In order to understand the siege as it really was we have to know that the seasons in Khartoum dominate life in the city. The great heat comes in March and is not relieved until rain falls, usually in July. By November the rains have stopped and cooler weather comes as a blessed relief in December. But the Nile falls rapidly when the rains cease, and the fall of the Nile was a major factor in the defence of Khartoum.[1]

Khartoum itself is tucked conveniently into the fork formed by the confluence of the White and Blue Niles. It is therefore defensible to the west by the White Nile, to the east by the Blue Nile and to the north by man-made ramparts linking the two rivers. Omdurman, on the other hand, which is linked to Khartoum so that they are two lungs of the same body, is on the west bank of the White Nile and so unprotected by water.

The Mahdi and his gigantic retinue, which swelled at times to a hundred thousand men, was always poised at El Obeid in Kordofan, some two hundred miles from Khartoum, deep in the desert which was his ally and his friend. The Mahdi felt safe in the desert. His camp was surrounded by rings of watchers in ever-widening circles who, by the telephony of the drums, could warn the camp of those who approached in a matter of minutes. It was a highly efficient, if primitive, system of military intelligence.

---

[1] Although the fall of the river is much the same each year, the date of its commencement and its pace vary greatly. This was to be a factor in the defence of Khartoum.

So just as the Nile was the friend and shield of Gordon, so the desert was the intimate and ally of the Mahdi. Neither man felt safe without the protection that these elements afforded. The Mahdi had the advantage of mobility. He could go where he liked, when he liked, at great speed. His horsemen and his camel-riders could survive in country and under conditions that would soon have killed the British soldier. While claustrophobia hung over Khartoum, the Mahdi's men in the open under the stars at night were buoyed up by the feeling that they were lords of the desert, and that the desert stretched right up to the very gateways of Omdurman, and also up to the ramparts of Khartoum. Long before the end came Gordon was the prisoner, the Mahdi the gaoler. Gordon did not keep a journal during the first months of the siege. Hope was high then. Gordon's mind was full of the political implications of relief. He was quite prepared to quit and let Zobeir take over as Governor-General with ample funds and fresh troops to oppose the Mahdi rebellion. If disasters came the Government could blame him. He would be the scapegoat if things went wrong. The Government would take the kudos if all turned out well.

On the 9th of September, the very day that Lord Wolseley landed in Cairo, Gordon sent his second-in-command Colonel Stewart, Frank Power *The Times* correspondent, and Monsieur Herbin the French Consul, down river to contact the relief force. With Stewart he sent all his reports on the situation as it really was, the dangers as well as the advantages he enjoyed. From that day until the 13th of December he wrote in his diary, putting down on paper the thoughts that raced through his mind, from the antics of a turkey-cock in the Palace courtyard to the most detailed preparations for the siege and defence of Khartoum.

Then for five weeks, to the end, we know nothing from his writings. Destitution, despair, and paralysing fear had Khartoum in its grip. What stands out in any close survey of the ten months of the siege of Khartoum is that Gordon, and Gordon alone, was the defender of the city. He had virtually no help. Stewart, until he left, was an able deputy, but to the people of Khartoum he was a nonentity. Only Gordon mattered. Gordon was watched constantly. His every look, gesture, word reported on and discussed to see if it could be interpreted as hope or despair. Gordon, whatever his personal feelings were, had to appear the embodiment of confidence. Always he must be the confident commander waiting for relief that was just round the corner. Never must he doubt in public. Only at night in the little bedroom he had constructed on the Palace roof, to catch whatever breeze might blow, could he relax. There, nightly, he was able to unburden his heart to God.

In the first few months after his arrival there was so much to be done that there was little time for contemplation. Gordon reinforced the Egyptian troops with slave levies who were trained and diociplinod until they were at least as reliable as the regulars. The Treasury ran out of cash. Gordon promptly ordered the printing of his own currency that had complete validity within the city. The troops required not only discipline but encouragement and Gordon, a great believer in medals for other men, had a series of medals struck for valour and for vigilance. He rationed the food supplies which could occasionally be supplemented by his steamers that were still able by keeping to midstream to chug along the Nile and make brief sorties ashore.

Gordon's gesture in allowing any who wished to join the Mahdi to leave had undoubtedly got rid of some potential saboteurs, but as the months dragged on the attitude of the populace, now feeling the first gnawing pangs of hunger, changed and became menacing. Ever on the look-out for revolt from within, Gordon seized two pashas and had them shot for sedition and conspiracy. The firm action quelled the discontent and treason in the city, but the death sentences preyed on Gordon's mind. He could act with swift decision and without doubting, but then came the post mortem. Was he justified in ordering a decapitation? Who but God Who gave life should take it? For weeks his prayers were haunted by these questions—and all the time the firm, resolute public image was maintained.

The chronicle of tragedy runs relentlessly through the story of the siege. In the first week in September Mahomet Ali, one of Gordon's most trusted commanders, although Gordon had told him never to leave the fortress of his steamer, foraged far inland

and was ambushed, losing his entire army of a thousand men. The Mahdi himself with his ever-increasing following was by this time slowly advancing on Khartoum from El Obeid. He was in no hurry. He was waiting for the Nile to go down until his dervishes could somewhere cross the moat that Gordon had built to link the two rivers. In October Ibrahim Rucdi, Gordon's trusted secretary, was found guilty of fraud and the theft of food. He was instantly dismissed and degraded.

In October Gordon received two letters from the Mahdi, one written in German by Slatin Pasha the Austrian who had fallen into the Mahdi's hands and been converted to Islam. The fact that Slatin had been taken prisoner, after putting up a stiff resistance, did not perturb Gordon, but his conversion aroused Gordon to anger. He always saw the clash in the Sudan as a struggle between the Christian faith and Islam, and for a Christian to become a Moslem was, Gordon thought, selling his soul. He sent the letters back unanswered.

Afterwards he relented a little and decided that, when it was all over, he would take Slatin with him to the Congo, for Gordon intended, after the relief of Khartoum, to cross over into the Congo and take up the appointment that the King of the Belgians was holding for him.

In the middle of October dreadful news came. The *Abbas*, a spy said, had been lost. Stewart, Power, and Herbin had been murdered. And Gordon's secret despatches to Cairo and London in which he revealed his plight had fallen into the hands of the Mahdi.

At first Gordon refused to believe that this could have happened. Even when the Mahdi, renewing his demand for surrender, quoted from the despatches, Gordon said it must be the work of a traitor who had informed the Mahdi of the despatches which he had somehow managed to read.

It was not until November that a letter from a Major Kitchener who was skirmishing well in advance of the main relieving force reached Gordon, confirming the loss of the *Abbas* and all those who had sailed in her. It was a crushing disaster. For now the Mahdi had real, reliable intelligence. He knew that Gordon was short of food, though not, of course, of water. He knew that the ammunition was low, and that morale was sustained by Gordon alone. From that moment the Mahdi must have known he could take Khartoum, but the rains had been heavy. The waters of the Nile receded very slowly, still protecting Gordon. It was not for another two months that the Mahdi struck. He had left it almost, but not quite, too late.

After the 14th of December we have no journal to guide us. For five weeks the little Englishman sustained the city. Food gave out. Horses were slaughtered for food. Birds, even rats, were eaten. Gordon contrived every kind of bluff to keep the Army at its post. Houses on the waterfront were prepared to receive the relief force. Rumours that the British were near were sedulously fanned and swept through the city. From the roof of the Palace the Governor-General, through his telescope, watched and watched. He watched the defences of Omdurman crumble when the ammunition over the river was exhausted. He watched his own men like a hawk, scanning their lines for any dereliction of duty. And, above all, he watched the bend in the river to the north around which, at any moment, he expected to see the relief flotilla steaming. He watched in vain. The tragedy of Khartoum, with the relentless certainty of great drama, was moving towards its bloody climax.

This was the siege in outline, but for us today it is relieved by many glimpses of General Gordon as he was, free of restricting discipline, free to put his unfettered thoughts on paper. Let us move into the Palace and share with Gordon for a time the routine of his daily life, his secret thoughts, and the hope and horror of his days.

In the first months he shared his life with Stewart and to a less extent with Frank Power, but when the *Abbas* left he was alone. He ate his meals alone in the great dining-room of the Palace with its portrait of the Khedive[1] gazing down on him. Six servants waited on him, but he ate and drank frugally, his mind always alive to the innumerable problems of the day. During these last lonely months his journal was his only companion. Into it he poured his views, his hopes, his strange erratic genius.

He refused to sleep in the four-poster bed that with its golden

[1] The portrait of Ismail had not been replaced by that of Tewfik.

panoply was the chief piece of furniture in the Governor-General's bedroom. He slept in the little temporary bedroom he had erected on the Palace roof. There he was not quite alone, for a guard was mounted night and day at the four corners of the roof and when the guard changed Gordon, without actually waking, knew what time it was—and if there was a disturbance either in the lines or in the city he knew that too. His secretary pointed out that the Palace roof was the most vulnerable place that the Governor-General could choose to sleep, but this did not deter Gordon. When the Mahdi moved his army over for the attack on Omdurman, one of his guns was brought down to the Nile daily to shell the Palace and any of Gordon's steamers that were within range, but at night there was little or no bombardment, and Gordon preferred the roof, which was several degrees cooler than the bedroom, and where he could—half asleep, half awake—be ready in a moment to deal with any surprise or crisis. So concentrated in his hands was the whole structure of the defence of Khartoum that he could not, he thought, afford the slumbrous security of a bedroom. He was much happier on the bridge with his guard and his telescopes.

There was certainly more than one telescope. Probably there were four, one at each corner of the roof, for they were heavy affairs weighing twenty pounds or more and it is unlikely that they were carried about as the situation demanded. One certainly was made by Chevalier of Paris and bought locally by Gordon. 'It is,' he said, 'the best glass I ever had.' But another was made by Callaghan and Company of New Bond Street, and it is still in good order today.

His telescopes were at this time a part of Gordon's life. He could watch the movements in the Mahdi's lines when the dervishes came within view. He could see his own lines, by the White Nile to the west, by the Blue Nile that flowed past to the east. He could see the deep moat he had dug to the south along which his own fortifications ran. One of his major anxieties was that with the falling Nile in the winter months this moat, which could not be made as deep as the river-beds, might dry up and let the dervishes come through. The Mahdi's men could always cross the White Nile higher up, and then in darkness approach these ramparts. If the moat dried up this was the weak spot in the defence. It worried Gordon who knew, with the trained mind of the engineer, just how grave the danger was.

He rose at dawn and drank a little tea before the sun, red and majestic, crept out of the east and, very soon it seemed, topped the coconut trees that fringed the river. Always the hawks were wheeling in their rhythmic circles even at dawn. They seemed like sentinels of the sky for ever on duty. Gordon wished that his own men were as diligent.

'Two sentries asleep spotted through the glass. Sent to have them thrashed. . . .' Gordon knew that he had to pounce on the first signs of disobedience in his ranks. He was greatly feared by everyone in the beleaguered city. Even the notables at the weekly meeting trembled in his presence. But Gordon comments that a little grey mouse had taken Stewart's place at his dining-table and, to Gordon's surprise, approached the Governor-General without any fear to be fed. The hungry mouse was but a sign of the times. Soon the people were to be hungry, too.

Always the problem of food—life itself—concerns him.

'3.30 p.m. Sentries off the roof of the North Fort again! Sent over to have them flogged.

'Rectified list of biscuits—266,430 okes.

'*Dhoora* in 2,100 *abeds* in magazine today. Six weeks' supply!'

The constant praying of the Arabs, both his own and the men of the Mahdi, was an unending feature of the scene from the Palace roof.

'No church parade to speak of. Arabs now only visible on the south front. They did not bring their gun down today. It's the Moslem sabbath [it was Friday the 19th of September] and there is no office work. Not that there is much on other days. One never sees anyone from morning till night.'

By 'anyone' he meant any other Englishman, someone he could talk to and trust. How much he would have appreciated at this time a companion. He was surrounded by dark faces and these faces he had to scan to detect whether the man still had courage or was cowardly, or was conceiving treachery. It was a nightmare of a life, but quietly lived by Gordon, alone, with only his faith to sustain him.

The tedium and the strain were relieved by amusing incidents.

'It is really amusing that (when one can scarcely call one's life one's own) one's servant, already with one wife—which most men find enough—asks for leave for three days to marry two more.

'The Arabs are firing their guns from Omdurman. They are also keeping up a musketry fire. At the Mahdi's camp another "Church Parade". I suppose they are working up their fanaticism. . . .'

That was just what in fact was happening. The Mahdi was in almost constant session with his three Kalifas and his Emirs. When the Mahdi learnt that the forces under General Stewart had inflicted a major defeat on the army of one of his allies, there was near panic in the Mahdi's camp.[1] But with the seizure of Gordon's private papers from the *Abbas* the Mahdi recovered his confidence. Even to the end the Mahdi himself had considerable misgivings about seizing Khartoum. Only the resolution of his Emirs, who pointed out that it was a heaven-sent opportunity, made him at last give his consent.

Gordon and the Mahdi were in touch with each other from time to time throughout the siege, and the meetings of the emissaries had an almost medieval flavour. As early as March, in response to Gordon's letter proposing peace and negotiated terms, the Mahdi had sent his messengers under the white flag to Gordon. Gordon received them in the great hall of the Palace wearing his wonderful Governor-General's coat, the one Ismail had given him. To Gordon's surprise one of the men produced a *jibbeh* and handed it to Gordon saying: 'Our master, the Mahdi, invites you to join the only true faith. . . .'

Gordon turned red at this insolence and threw the *jibbeh* with a gesture of disgust on the floor. It is hardly to be wondered at that nothing came of the meeting.

When the Mahdi had translated and read the papers from the *Abbas* and knew Gordon's plight his tone became more threatening:

[1] On the 2nd of January, Sir Hubert Stewart (not related to the Colonel Stewart who had been murdered on the *Abbas*) had defeated an Arab force at Abu Klea Wells, near Korte, killing over a thousand Arabs for the loss of less than two hundred men.

'To Gordon Pasha of Khartoum. May God guide him into the path of virtue! Amen.

'Know that your small steamer the *Abbas* has been captured by the will of God. Those who believed in us as Mahdi have been saved, but those who did not were destroyed, even as the Consuls and others on board.'

The Mahdi then quoted in detail from Gordon's private despatches and ended with the menacing threat that surrender, after battle, 'would not be accepted'. The hint was plain.

Gordon never yielded an inch in his negotiations with the Mahdi after his original offer of peace was rejected. He never threatened. But his attitude clearly showed that he believed help was at hand and that swift retribution would overtake his enemy. It was Gordon's stout refusal to negotiate any terms of surrender that made the Mahdi so hesitant to attack.

Kitchener's message had heartened Gordon and Gordon actually wrote a minute that suggested that Kitchener should be the new Governor-General of the Sudan. To suggest that a major on active service should hold this post was probably the most amazing piece of intuition that Gordon ever achieved. He had in a marked degree the flair for intuitive interpretation, of the present and of the future, that distinguishes the truly great leader from the intellectual leader or from the man who has reached his position of command by hard work and promotion alone.

The fall of Omdurman was terrible news. It was only just over the river, but when the commander signalled to Gordon that he had not one round of ammunition left Gordon was compelled to reply that he should surrender.

The Mahdi's men were all around now, pressing Khartoum like the angry teeth of a rapidly closing vice.

Still Gordon performed his daily round of the lines, the arsenal, the steamers, the granary, and the barracks. Without his daily personal presence Khartoum would collapse. With him the defence was sustained.

In January the Nile, at last, started to fall rapidly. Every morning Gordon would inspect the measure stake on the water-front outside the Palace entrance. Every day the Nile had dropped inches, and the rate of the fall increased daily. That ditch to the

M

south was becoming dry now, and the dry bed firm enough to hold the Mahdi's men if they did attack. Gordon marvelled that the Mahdi delayed so long. 'It really looks as if *he* might be too late,' he wrote in the first week in December.

On the 14th of December the *Bordein* was sent down river under heavy gunfire with a few refugees and some despatches including the journal. In the last hastily written note Gordon complained with some bitterness: 'You send me no information, though you have lots of money.'

They were the last words of Gordon to the outside world.

But Khartoum was to hold out for another five weeks during which the starving people were eating rats, mice, snakes, anything that came their way. The dead lined the streets and the odour of death hung heavy over the city.

Early in the morning of the 26th of January, before dawn, the Mahdi's dervishes,[1] who had crossed the Nile in silence and in secrecy during the night in great numbers, attacked the moat and ramparts to the south. The moat bed was hard-baked by the sun and held the swarming black feet of the Arabs.

Gordon, in his fitful sleep on the Palace roof, instantly awoke as the tumult of fighting and firing in the lines, not three miles away, broke out. He tried to discover what had happened. It was too late. The Mahdi's men, screaming, killing all who stood in their path, men, women, and children, burning the houses, had stormed through the lines in one blind, ferocious charge which carried them to the gates of the Palace. Gordon heard the cries: 'To the Palace! To the Palace!' The leaders urging on their men.

At the Palace gates they halted, fearing mines. Gordon had helped to fire a gun from the Palace roof until the trajectory became too acute and he could no longer train his weapon on the attacking mob. But by this time the dervishes were mad with murder and loot.

Before they had attacked that morning the Mahdi had promised them Paradise or victory. Now they ignored any mines that might be ready to explode in their faces. They swarmed over the Palace fence and rushed to the main white-marble stairway.

When Gordon had found that he could no longer fire the

---

[1] The correct name for the followers of the Mahdi was—and still is—*Ansar*.

roof-gun he went to his room, changed quickly into his Governor-General's uniform, and for the first time for many years, took a revolver in one hand and a sword in the other.

There are several accounts of what happened then. I prefer the one that says he walked down the steps into the oncoming dervishes, firing with his revolver as he went, killing the spearmen in his path and then, the chamber of his revolver exhausted, used his sword to attack his tormentors.

It was all in vain, of course. The heavy spears of the dervishes, some with their blades corrugated so that they could not be withdrawn without tearing out the flesh of the victim, were hurled into him with fanatical force and accuracy.

His head was cut off and carried in triumph to the Mahdi at Omdurman. His body lay rotting in the sun where it was mutilated by a thousand passing spearmen. Then, a tangled, bloody carcass in ribbons, it was thrown into a well.

Gordon was dead. He died, as he lived, unafraid.

20

The Legend Lives

Two days after Gordon's death[1] the advance guard of Wolseley's army, a flotilla under the command of Sir Charles Wilson, rounded the bend of the river and, running through a barrage of gun- and rifle-fire from the shore, came into sight of Gordon's Palace. For miles the natives on the banks had shouted to them that they were too late, but they could not believe it. England was tense for the relief of Gordon. His name was on everyone's lips, from the Queen to the dock workers in Woolwich and Gravesend. In anticipation of the relief of Khartoum *Punch* had even printed a cartoon of the scene entitled: 'At last!'

So Wilson and his men could not believe their eyes. They sent a party ashore at great risk. The men confirmed the news. The Mahdi was now King, his Kalifas great men, his Emirs seizing all the best houses for their innumerable households. Wilson had to retreat and he had great difficulty in doing so. He was harried and harassed all the way down river, a continuous fusillade of shots, night and day, made navigation extremely difficult. He was lucky to survive.

The news reached Britain and the shock was cataclysmic. To a great, growing, aggressive power that believed without doubting in its mission it was a humiliating, almost incredible, blow to prestige and national feeling. Then as now, of course, there was a vociferous minority to whom their country was always wrong, the

[1] The 28th of January, Gordon's fifty-second birthday.

enemy always right. These people, in and out of Parliament, pretended to rejoice at the fall of Khartoum and British Imperialism. But the people as a whole knew that greatness could not tolerate this kind of reverse. The Queen was, in this, by instinct and by training, at one with her people. Her anger knew no bounds.

'How shall I attempt to express *what I feel?*' she wrote to Gordon's sister. 'To think of your dear, noble, heroic brother who served his country and his Queen so truly, so heroically . . . not having been rescued. That the promises of support were not fulfilled is grief inexpressible.'

And if Mr Gladstone should come to hear of the contents of the letter so much the better. The Queen's contempt for her Prime Minister was no secret now.

Miss Gordon, thanking the Queen for her letter, sent her one of Gordon's bibles. It is still at Windsor Castle.

Meanwhile the Mahdi had been reasserting his authority after the looting and ravaging of the city of Khartoum. It was not an easy matter. The dervishes had tasted blood and they liked the taste of blood and torture. They revelled in the rape of the women, and if these women were Greek nuns their shrieks of protest, their prayers, and their pleas only added to the fun. For forty-eight hours the city was given over to a reign of terror and orgy. Then the Mahdi, who had established his entourage at Omdurman, crossed the river and personally ordered the arson, the looting, and the raping to stop. Khartoum gradually began to struggle back to life again with the Arabs in the great houses instead of the Egyptians and the foreigners.

The taking and sacking of Khartoum was the greatest victory that Islam could claim over Christianity for a hundred years. The Mahdi felt himself to be a despot whose word was law and whose writ ran as far as his armies could march. The Anglo-Egyptian forces were soon back defensively on the Wadi Halfa lines, for the British Government had refused to allow Wolseley to go on and avenge Gordon. Osman Dinga, that durable rebel, seized all the Red Sea Hills except the little trading and slaving port of Suakin, to which the British clung tenaciously. Emin, who held out in the deep south, was driven back almost to the Great Lakes.

A million square miles or more was Mahdi territory, and for thirteen years the Mahdi and his successors were to rule a purely Arab state by Arab methods. That meant an absolute despotism. The Mahdi himself saw to his secret police, who informed him of everything that was happening, even in Kordofan, even on the Red Sea coast. He executed, he tortured, and he mutilated any suspected of disloyalty, but he did set up a stable, workable native state, in which the ordinary people were no more unhappy than they had been under the Egyptians. As it happened, the Mahdi was not to enjoy his creation for more than six months after Gordon's death. How he died is a mystery. He may have been poisoned. Not everyone loved the Mahdi, but it is more likely he died of a fever, perhaps smallpox, his constitution undermined by the fact that after the fall of Khartoum he had given himself over to a continuous debauchery with his hundreds of new wives: African, Egyptian, Turkish, Armenian. They were of all ages from seven to seventeen, and they took it in turns to venerate and titillate the gross fat figure of the Mahdi as he lounged on his divan between the hours of prayer which he still kept. He still put on his patched *jibbah* when walking to the mosque through the crowd who still venerated him, kissing the earth he had trodden on so that some of his immaculate holiness might be imparted to them.

The Mahdi's death did not upset the stability of the tight autocracy that had been erected. The Kalifa Abdulla was chosen to succeed him, and the Mahdi's state went from strength to strength. In one matter the Mahdi had been disappointed: he had not wanted Gordon killed.[1] Gordon, dead, was no use to him. Alive he would have been the best possible hostage. He could have joined Slatin, whom the Mahdi was still keeping as a privileged slave, who had always to be in attendance on his master, crawling to him when ordered, running by his horse when the Mahdi travelled, or sitting cross-legged near his master in the mosque. Slatin eventually escaped. He must often have wished he had died before that day arrived.

The Kalifa Abdulla was no nonentity. He was as strong and resolute and as ingenious as the Mahdi had been. He did not have

---

[1] The present Mahdi confirmed this to the author in Khartoum in 1961.

that sweet, magnetic smile, nor that gift for inspiring absolute devotion, but he was a statesman of real ability.

He carried on the Mahdi's tradition of writing letters to the European monarchs suggesting that they should join Islam before it was too late. Three envoys of Abdulla arrived in Cairo bearing three such letters. One was addressed to His Highness the Khedive, one to the Sultan of Turkey, and one to Her Britannic Majesty Queen Victoria. After considerable consultation all the letters were returned unanswered, but with a message saying that all the monarchs would not deign to reply. In London, and even in Constantinople, it was easy to laugh at the pretensions of this preposterous Arab ruler, but in Cairo it was not quite so easy. The Mahdi's state was aggressive everywhere. The black flag of the Mahdi and his Kalifas inspired terror in all who had not already become followers. At one time the Mahdi's men penetrated fifty miles into Egypt and the Khedive did not appear to be able to do anything effective in reply. Mahdism was a real menace to Africa. There was nowhere an army to oppose the Mahdi's *ansars*, or dervishes, as the British called them.

The turn of history came in 1895, when a Tory government turned out the Liberal administration. The British public had never ceased to long for revenge. The memory of that disaster must be wiped out. This was still the overwhelming feeling of the British people. It was grotesque that the greatest empire the world had ever seen should be defied by one Arab despotism that constantly insulted, imprisoned, or killed any white man who tried to live in the Sudan.

Young Major Herbert Kitchener, now a general at forty-eight, was chosen to lead the expedition. He was the ideal leader of a giant punitive expedition. He was ruthless, domineering, ambitious, and resolute. But he was a born commander. His army, that in the end numbered over twenty thousand men, marched slowly up the Nile. At Atbara they defeated decisively an Arab force sent down to meet them under the Emir Mahmoud. And, on the 1st of September 1898, before Omdurman, Kitchener contrived the greatest slaughter of an Arab army that the world had witnessed. Eight thousand dead were left on the field. Kitchener lost less than three hundred men.

Men who have become famous in our own day took part in the battle: Beatty the sailor and Churchill the soldier were there, the latter wisely changing his sword for a revolver at the last moment. The Mahdi's hordes had no fear. They advanced on the British guns like a moving mountain of black humanity. They were mown down without compunction. British rule in the Sudan —though in nominal co-partnership with Egypt[1]—was established until the granting of independence to the new Sudan on the 1st of January 1956.

All Gordon's prophecies came true. If you do not act now, he had said, you will have to act later and on a much more serious scale. So it happened. Even his suggestion that young Kitchener should be appointed Governor-General came true. He installed himself in the reconstructed Palace after telling his officers to 'loot like mad' to furnish the Palace with suitable grandeur.

The Queen, of course, was delighted. She was very old now, but when her lady-in-waiting read her the news from *The Times* she wept with pride and relief. She had seen her empire grow and grow. She was Empress of India, the matriarch of Europe, and now, in all but name, Queen of most of Africa. And Gordon, dearly beloved General Gordon, had been avenged at last.

So Christianity, for a time, triumphed over Islam. One speculates as to what Charles Gordon would have thought of it all. Gordon was not by nature an Imperialist. He was in a sense the best servant that Islam ever had. He was loyal to the Khedive, at least as loyal as he was to Baring. He did not believe that it was the British mission to conquer, certainly not to oppress. He liked people to have a say in their own destiny. But in the manner of his day Gordon believed that Britain had much to offer Islamic countries, and all African countries, that they were unlikely to get elsewhere. Although this is now unfashionable thinking it was true at the time. The British seconded officers were for the most part scrupulously honest and fair. Neither the Portuguese nor the French could claim as much for their men. On these simple qualities the immense prestige of Britain in

---

[1] After a mutiny of Egyptian troops in Khartoum in 1925 Britain ruled, and there was co-dominance only in name. The Egyptian claim to the Sudan was re-asserted by King Farouk before his abdication. Now there are said to be 'friendly' relations between the two states.

Africa—which still persists in spite of modern trends—was founded. The Sudan was built up into a new, modern homogeneous state by a small body of British civil servants who for very small salaries gave the people—the illiterate, industrious *fellahin*, the workers—what they had never had before and could never hope to have from any other source: a fair deal, legal rights as well as duties, the protection of the rule of law, manhood in its most essential form. Slavery, in all its guises, was at last wiped out of the Nile Valley.

And what, after a lapse of nearly eighty years, are we to say of Charles Gordon?

He must at times have been an infuriating subordinate. He was swayed by his emotions. He was volatile and quick-tempered. He was consumed at times by a spiritual struggle that was carried on in secret till the day of his death and did not make him any easier to live with. He was not even bound by the conventional loyalties that we accept today. He was quite prepared, if he quarrelled with the British Government, to go off and serve the King of the Belgians, though one must admit that there would have been some surprises in store for that monarch if Gordon had ever got control of his Congolese empire. History might have had a different page to write. Under Gordon the Congo would have had a liberal tutor in an age when liberalism and Imperialism did not walk hand in hand.

One of the signs of Gordon's magnetism, and perhaps of his greatness, was and is that, however wrong he was at any given moment, one is always inclined to take his side and not the side of bureaucratic logic. Gordon in life and in death is irresistible.

When one compares Gordon's character with that of Kitchener one sees the difference between erratic genius and great ability and ambition. Kitchener accepted the Victorian values. He loved the houses of the rich, the great, the powerful. Gordon had no time for them. Kitchener loved grandeur, pomp, ceremony—the outward, visible signs of victory and power. Gordon was never happier than when he was exerting his authority without any of the appendages of greatness.

Was he a happy man? Perhaps not. His spirit was too turbulent for happiness. The Sudan excited him and the Nile became almost a mother to him, until that last fateful winter when her waters fell too far. But he does not seem to have been happy in the Sudan except, perhaps, during his first three years as Governor of Equatoria, when he was entirely his own master after he had arranged direct communication with the Khedive by circumventing the Governor-General in Khartoum.

But perhaps if Gordon had been asked to name the period of his life when he had felt most serene it would have been the seven years as a serving officer in Gravesend, when there was no fame or publicity at all. It was then that his interest in young people who were handicapped by social conditions really had a chance to bear fruit. And it was then that he had the unexacting daily routine of a serving officer.

The work he did for boys who were, he said, England in the making has not been forgotten, for the very good reason that it still lives. Khartoum University is founded on the rock of Gordon College which was felt at the time to be the natural way to perpetuate his name. And in Britain Gordon Boys' School in Surrey carries on Gordon's name, Gordon's life, and the kind of ideals in which, simply, Gordon believed. The boys wear a uniform made of the Gordon tartan, and their training is the kind of faith that Gordon had: belief in service to the community and the country. It is not unfitting that the Queen, the great, great grand-daughter of Victoria, should be the school's patron. In the school's museum are all the relics of Gordon. His mandarin's jacket, his journal, the tongs he brightened his fire with in Gravesend, all are there. They make him live again.

When one writes of Gordon, even at this distance of time, it is as if he were looking over one's shoulder.

'I can't really take the credit for that,' he seems to be saying, 'I just happened to be there at the right time.'

His contempt and indeed dislike of money, his incorrigible flair for saying the right thing at the wrong time, his tempers and his tantrums, his inward battle to be the kind of man with whom he could live in peace, his outlandish intuition—these were but a part of him.

Above and beyond all the qualities and failings, there was in him always a great compassion and a light of leadership that nothing could extinguish.

As long as there are men and women in Britain and her Commonwealth who are proud of the British story, the legend of Charles Gordon will live on.

Bibliography

I have had access to a large number of papers and letters dealing with the varied aspects of the life of Gordon. Among the many books I have consulted are:

WILSON: *Colonel Gordon's Chinese Campaign*

HAKE: *The Story of Chinese Gordon*

FORBES: *Chinese Gordon*

WILSON: *The Ever Victorious Army*

BOULGER: *Life of Gordon*

LILLEY: *General Gordon at Gravesend*

GORDON: *Letters of General Gordon to his sister*

MOSSMAN: *Gordon's Diary*

SETON CHURCHILL: *Gordon, The Christian Hero*

GRANT: *The War in the Sudan*

GILLIAT: *Heroes of Modern Crusades*

HILL: *Gordon in Central Africa*

FRANK POWER: *Letters from Khartoum*

HAKE: *Gordon's Journals*

ELTON: *Gordon's Khartoum Journals*

ALFORD AND SWORD: *The Egyptian Sudan Gordon Pasha of the Sudan French*
(Facsimile)(Kegan Paul): *General Gordon's Last Journal*

MOOREHEAD: *The White Nile*

QUILLER COUCH: *The Roll of Honour*

Index